PRAISE FOR *LEADERSHIP IS PERSONAL*

Brad Mahon is a true authentic leader. In his presence you feel heard, appreciated, and valued. In this important book, he outlines how he has become that leader through relatable stories, anecdotes, and reading he has engaged in over the last two decades. Reading this book feels like sitting down with a knowledgeable friend who understands you, lifts you up, and challenges you to think differently about yourself as a leader.

—Krissy Collins
Dean, Division of Continuing Education, University of California, Irvine

Brad Mahon is one of the up-and-coming leaders in higher education in Canada today. Authenticity is the hallmark of the leadership style that has contributed to his success. His reflections on leadership are a great resource for anyone traveling their own leadership path.

—Mark Frison
President, Assiniboine College; President Emeritus, Great Plains College

Embracing the message of this timely book won't just add value to your business—it will add value to your life!

Brad Mahon nails the critical gaps between leadership and value-driven leadership. *Leadership Is Personal* will have you positively assessing the level of depth in which your values influence and engage others around you; it will have you racing into the world to be a value-driven leader on your path to personal and professional success.

Your status quo will be challenged, but as this driven leader and author points out, "A leader must be able to share their values. What they are and why they matter to them."

—Greg Gutek
President, Partners Development Group

Leadership books like this one act as a North Star, guiding us toward authentic leadership. Brad demonstrates his understanding and passion for continuous self-improvement, inviting readers to explore their own journey by nurturing their emotional intelligence. This book is not just a recipe; it's Brad's outlook on life, reminding us that true leadership requires ongoing work and self-reflection.

—Deron Bilous, ECA, MBA
Senior Vice President, Western Canada, Counsel Public Affairs

In this book, Dr. Brad Mahon shares insights from his personal experience as he shares thoughts and ideas for becoming a successful business leader. The discipline and compassion necessary to become a musician and teacher have been reflected in Brad's various management roles. His invitation for the reader to look inward first sets the stage for the journey that follows. As a Discipline Specialist for The Royal Conservatory of Music, Brad has supported and nurtured other colleagues' talents, while always leading by example. This book is a must read for all who are interested in developing and refining their leadership skills!

—Elaine Rusk

Vice President, Academics and Publishing, The Royal Conservatory of Music

LEADERSHIP
IS PERSONAL

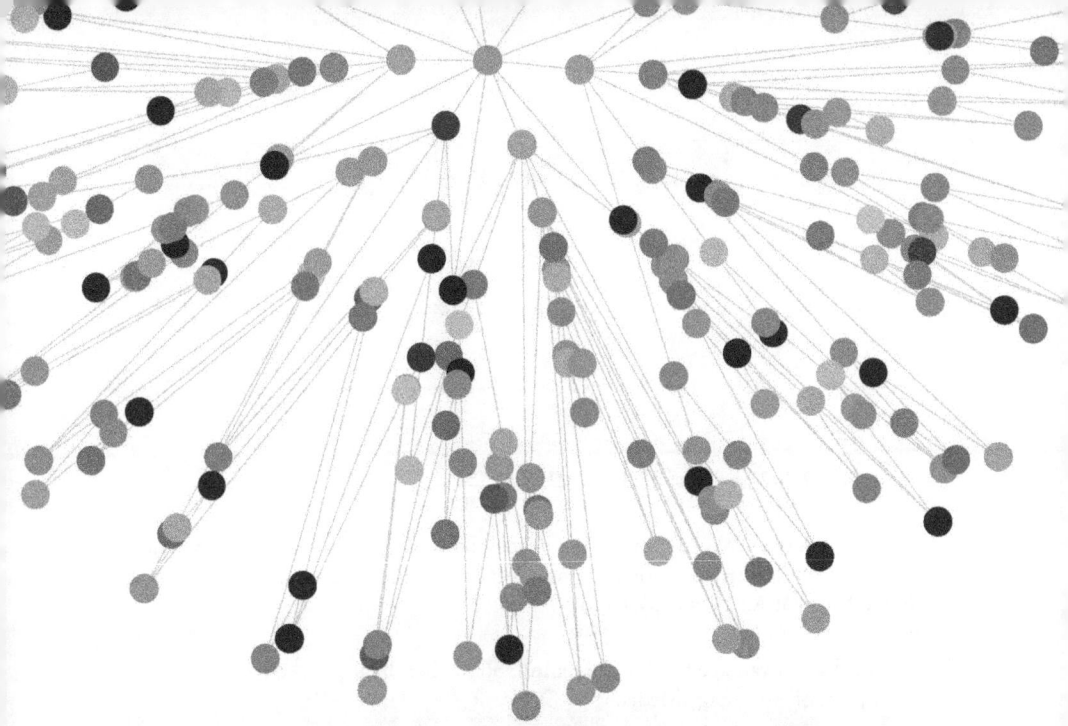

LEADERSHIP
IS PERSONAL

HOW COMMUNITY AND CULTURE

LEAD TO BUSINESS SUCCESS

BRAD MAHON

MBA, PhD

Advantage | Books

Published by Advantage Books, Charleston, South Carolina.
An imprint of Advantage Media.

ADVANTAGE is a registered trademark, and the Advantage colophon is a trademark of Advantage Media Group, Inc.

Printed in the United States of America.

10 9 8 7 6 5 4 3 2 1

ISBN: 979-8-89188-071-9 (Paperback)
ISBN: 979-8-89188-072-6 (eBook)

Library of Congress Control Number: 2024922193

Cover design by Matthew Morse.
Layout design by Ruthie Wood.

This publication is designed to provide accurate and authoritative information in regard to the subject matter covered. It is sold with the understanding that the publisher is not engaged in rendering legal, accounting, or other professional services. If legal advice or other expert assistance is required, the services of a competent professional person should be sought.

Advantage Books is an imprint of Advantage Media Group. Advantage Media helps busy entrepreneurs, CEOs, and leaders write and publish a book to grow their business and become the authority in their field. Advantage authors comprise an exclusive community of industry professionals, idea-makers, and thought leaders. For more information go to **advantagemedia.com**.

For those who have mentored me, and each colleague and partner I've had the privilege of working with—in appreciation for your trust and camaraderie.

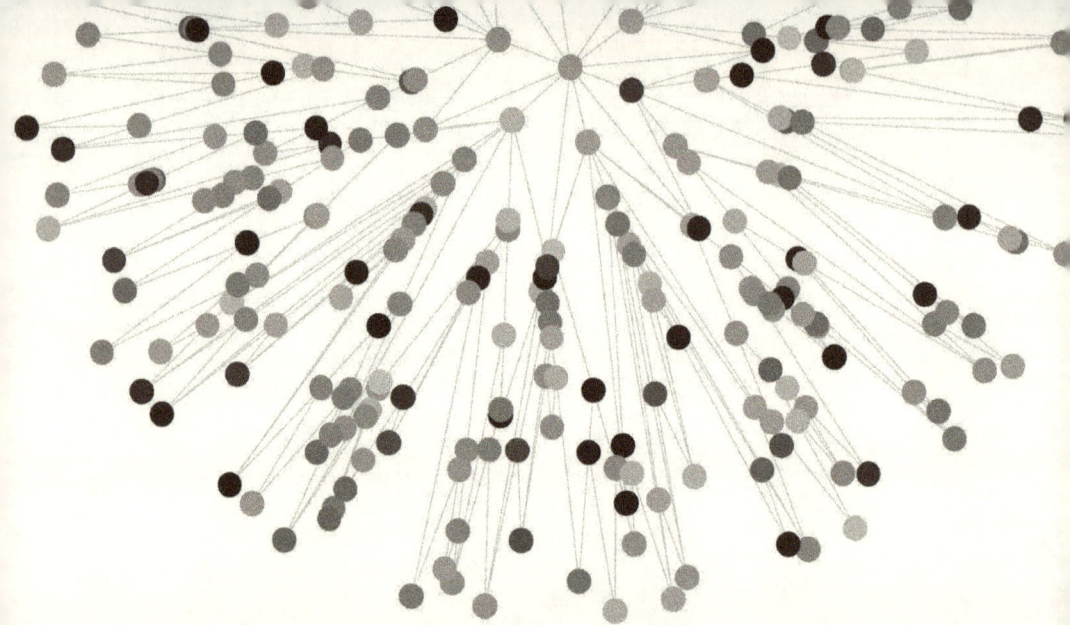

CONTENTS

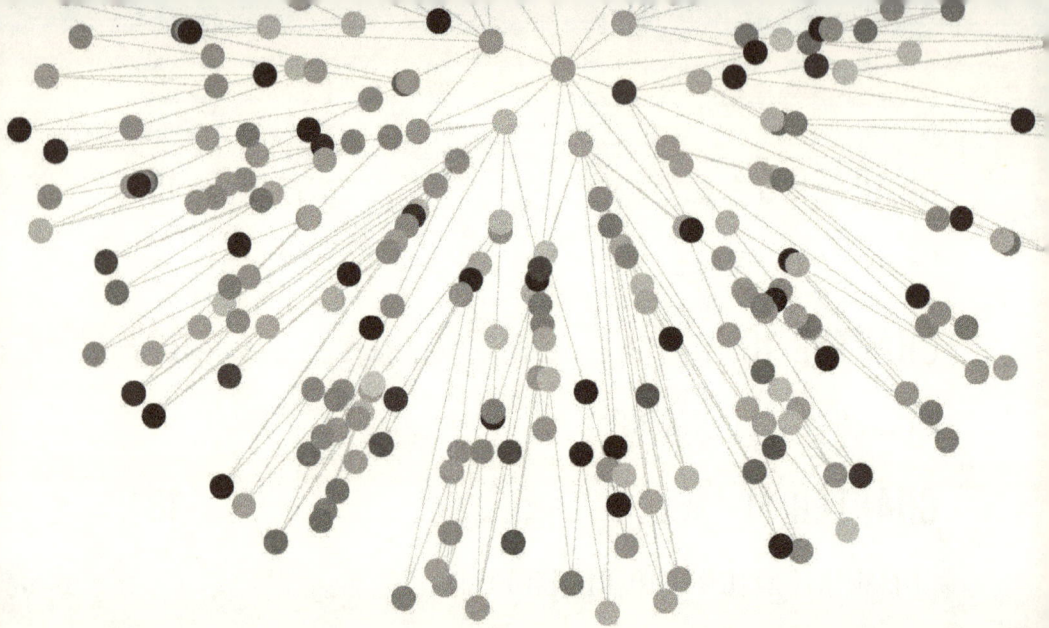

ACKNOWLEDGMENTS

I am sincerely grateful to Lindsey McCoy, Kristen Hackler, Katie Smith, Annie LaGreca, and the team at Advantage Media and Forbes Books.

Writing coach Anthony Noel helped me clarify my messages and see my story through the reader's eyes. I appreciate Tony's patience and grace, despite his questionable taste in sports teams.

This book would not have happened without the constant support of my family, especially my wife, Jade.

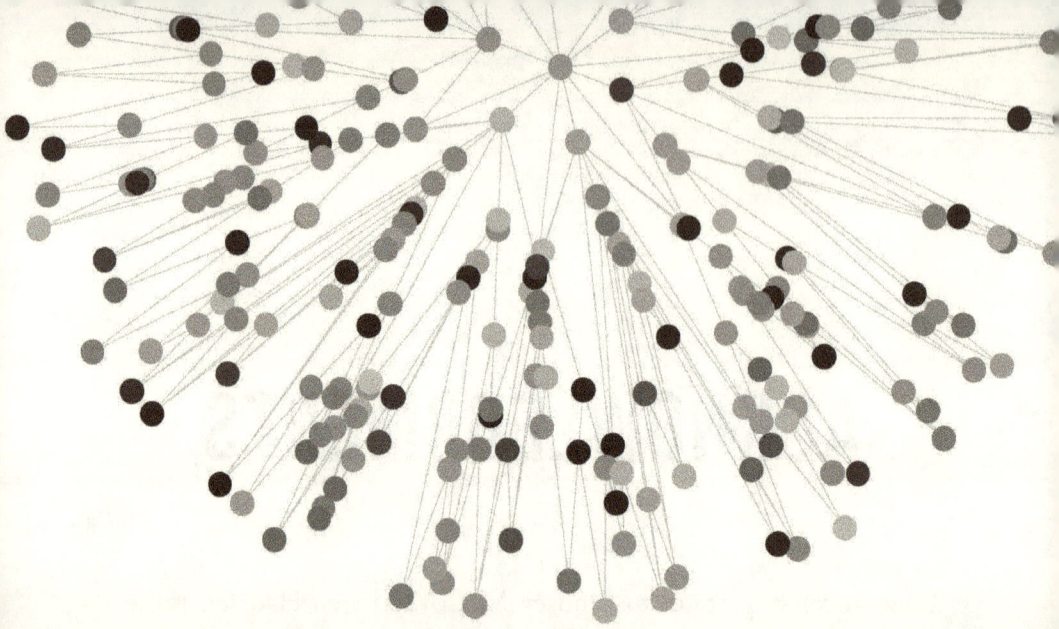

ABOUT THE AUTHOR

Brad Mahon, MBA, PhD, has enjoyed more than twenty-five years as a leader in higher education. His experience spans from the classroom to the boardroom, always with an emphasis on engaging the community.

As a college president (and past university dean), he passionately advocates for providing learners with transformative educational experiences and aligning institutions with the communities they serve. Collaboration and cooperation are hallmarks of his administrative tenures, including establishing strategic partnerships with other educational institutions, community organizations, and industry.

When no one is looking, Brad still sneaks off campus to moonlight as a freelance professional guitarist.

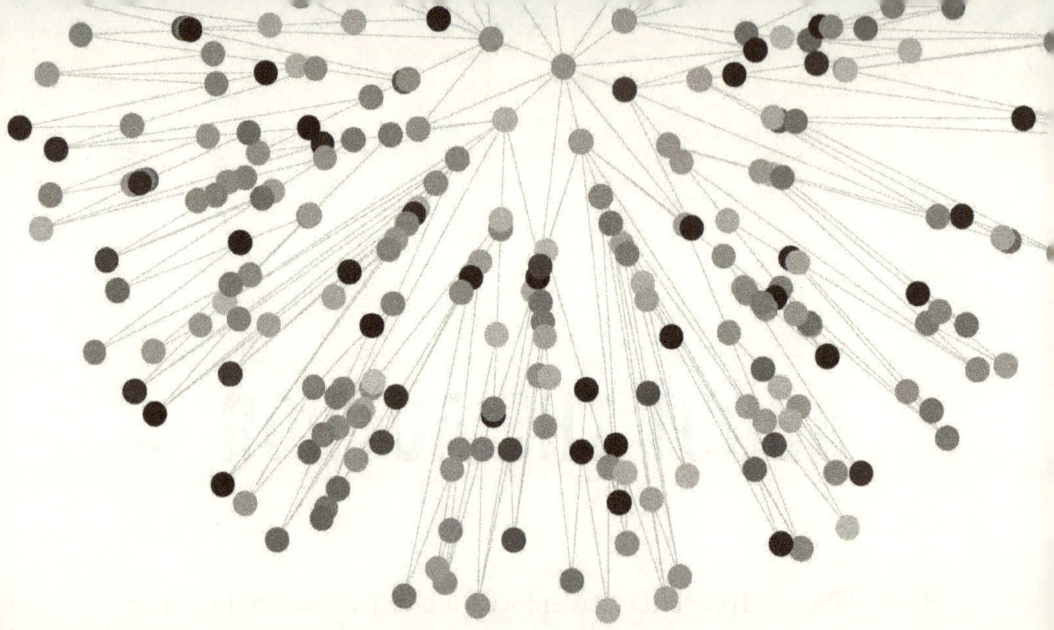

INTRODUCTION

WHY COMMUNITY ENGAGEMENT MATTERS

Authority is not leadership.

—MARK CARNEY[1]

It was my first year as president at Grasslands College, and I'd been looking forward to this day since taking the job. The campus buzzed as attendees mingled at our major yearly fundraising event.

Even before my official first day in the role, I had spent time in the community, getting to know my new city and its residents. People responded enthusiastically when I introduced myself as the new college president, many connecting the college with this annual fundraiser.

The positive mentions of this event increased after my tenure officially began, with several people declaring our fundraiser *the* community event of the year. And now—surreally, on one level—it was here.

---

1   Carney, M. (2021). *Values: Building a better world for all.* Signal.

I had come a long way. (You will learn about my journey throughout the following chapters.)

Almost a year into my role, I had a good handle on who was who, both on campus and in the community. As I circulated and spoke to guests, a revelation struck: our *entire community* surrounded me. Students and alumni. Faculty and staff. Donors and sponsors. Business owners and community leaders. Municipal, provincial, and federal government officials. And most telling of this event's reach were *those who had none of these official connections to, or histories with, our college.* This event was their only regular interaction with us.

Maybe—I chuckled inside—*that's because it was a high-profile, fun event—and there'd be no test at the end of the evening!*

The local media attended, took some photos, and asked a few questions. The reporter noted that the event was sold out and wondered if the college might consider moving it to a larger venue—a place where we could perhaps double our attendees. "Absolutely not," I was quick to reply.

While I took his point about the potential for increasing attendance (and thereby, donations), part of the event's value, I said, was having the community *on* our campus. For that one night, our college was *the* place to be; *we* were the city's main attraction.

I reflected on the power of community engagement. This event was gratifying, and only affirmed the positive outcomes I'd valued and worked toward—along with many, many teammates—across my career.

A career that, in hindsight, has followed an unexpected and crooked path.

My First Business Deal

Like millions of kids around the world, my first guitar was an air guitar.

Leaping from his bed, Teenage Brad crashed to the floor, magnifying the climactic downbeat that starts the final chorus of "Rock and Roll All Nite." Once I finished "performing" the entire KISS *Alive!* album,[2] I offered my imaginary audience an encore via the complete *Alive II* sequel.[3] Eventually, I advanced to the tennis racket—its shape a perfect stand-in for a guitar's body, and *it had strings*!

After hundreds of such (magnificent, if I say so myself) performances, air guitar and tennis racket were no longer enough; I had to "get inside" this music.

Serendipitously, I'd been grounded for a significant period. So at the age of thirteen, I set about negotiating my first business deal: *full compliance* with that punishment in exchange for an electric guitar and amplifier. My parents' counteroffer was an insistence that I take lessons and commit to regular practice—and just like that, the deal was done, and my life's course was set.

I didn't end up selling out clubs on LA's Sunset Strip but did make noise in some local bars, found my way into music school (plan B), collected some paperwork, and settled into a teaching job at the local college to supplement my guitarist-for-hire gigs.

Leadership was never part of the plan; it was an accident.

Or was it?

Becoming a Spartan

Back when I was ten years old, I sat cross-legged in our school's large, open carpeted area—where our school community came together.

It was the year-end assembly, and our principal, Mr. Walters, was addressing the students. Startled from yet another daydream, I heard

---

2   KISS. (1975). *Alive!* Casablanca.

3   KISS. (1977). *Alive II.* Casablanca.

him call my name. Friends smiled and gave me playful, supportive nudges, so I figured whatever Mr. Walters had said was positive.

As attention shifted to the next name called, what was happening finally dawned on me: I had been named one of several team captains for next year's school intramurals.

Mr. Walters was passionate about history, especially ancient Greece, and our school teams were named Athens, Rome, Sparta, and Troy. I was named house leader of Team Sparta.

I worked up the courage that summer to finally ask Mr. Walters what a house leader did when I was at his house hanging out with his son, Brian. I wasn't the best student, but I always tried harder for Mr. Walters, because I liked him—an early leadership realization. I didn't want to disappoint him but didn't know why he picked me.

My question was met with surprise that quickly turned to enthusiasm and warmth.

"I want *you* to be *you*," he explained. "I want you to help others, especially the younger kids. Encourage them, teach them, and show them, through your actions."

I processed his words for the rest of the summer and still think about them today.

It was an early lesson for Little Brad—a pivotal experience that shaped my views on leadership, culture, and community. I realized that it sometimes takes others to recognize and remind us of our gifts and how we can contribute.

There were other early lessons too.

Teenage Brad ran for class president and won. My "critical" duties included organizing the year-end pool party. University Brad was the student representative on Faculty Council. At the time, I never saw these as leadership roles. It was service.

Only later would I connect the dots: *leadership is service.*

An Accidental Leader

Fast-forward: How did I trade the concert stage's limelight for the boardroom's fluorescents?

I went from aspiring/wannabe rock star and college music student to professional guitarist-for-hire and college instructor before joining "the dark side": administration.

My career compounded organically. As my desk duties grew, teaching and playing shrank. I went from program coordinator to department head, to manager, to director, to dean, to president.

It's funny; I needed a PhD to teach in postsecondary classrooms, but *no formal training* was required to lead people and run a business or school! I often felt like I was making it up as I went along.

With some experience—and much reflection—I recognized that my life's journey had provided me with tools and lessons to build on. I became aware of my transferable skills and natural competencies. Still, I "went back" and filled in the gaps, completing an MBA in executive management in my forties. So many things clicked as I complemented my intuition and experience with theory and best practices.

This book is a reflection on my life's successes *and* failures. I'll share key realizations about authenticity, people-centric leadership, and community engagement that have fueled my success.

WHY THIS BOOK?

Anyone who studies lean philosophy knows its lessons are transferable. Strategies from Toyota's plant floors, including the fundamental lean idea of *kaizen*, or continual improvement, are relatable principles regardless of the sector.[4]

---

4   Dennis, P. (2017). *Lean production simplified: A plain-language guide to the world's most powerful production system*. CRC Press.

Part of my journey and quest for continuous improvement has been to consistently reflect, learn, and grow, and that is what I offer in these pages. Through my words and real-world examples, I hope to help those leading a team of one or many, a small business or a large company, in urban and rural settings alike.

This book distills hard-won lessons so readers can achieve similar benefits in their organizations. If there's one thing I know for sure, it's that *success can be studied and duplicated*. What I've achieved is teachable.

My core premise? Community engagement and corporate culture drive business success.

In treating my college and university posts as a business manager—such as believing that education is my product and students are clients that have choices—I've made community engagement my differentiator, my competitive advantage. The results have been happier customers, enhanced organizational reputations, greater brand awareness, heightened partnerships, improved employee satisfaction, and healthier financial positions.

> **COMMUNITY ENGAGEMENT AND CORPORATE CULTURE DRIVE BUSINESS SUCCESS.**

Our world demands instant gratification, and that's not an opinion; it's reality. Whatever the product or desired outcome—including success—people want what they want *now*. Just look around. Examples come from sports, entertainment, and business. *Consumers lack patience.*

It's no surprise, then, that we've never had more options—a myriad of alternatives to whatever is being sold and consumed. Leaders must, therefore, succeed *quickly*, and *new* leaders enjoy little margin for error.

What's Ahead

This book focuses on three things: self-leadership, external community, and internal culture.

In part 1, we begin by developing the self-awareness leaders require for success through internal reflection and self-discovery—identifying your values, finding your voice, and creating your vision.

Part 2 turns outward—making connections, assessing your community, and building partnerships. In part 3, I address culture within our organizations—hiring practices, communication, and modeling organizational values.

My fundamental messages are:

LEAD FROM WITHIN. TRUE LEADERSHIP STEMS FROM SELF-AWARENESS, EMOTIONAL INTELLIGENCE, AND CLEARLY DEFINED VALUES THAT GUIDE YOUR VISION AND VOICE. BY DOING THE INNER WORK FIRST, YOU CAN LEAD WITH AUTHENTICITY AND PURPOSE.

CONNECT WITH YOUR COMMUNITY. ORGANIZATIONS AND LEADERS MUST MOVE BEYOND A TRANSACTIONAL MINDSET AND FULLY ENGAGE THEIR COMMUNITIES. UNDERSTANDING YOUR NEIGHBORS, FORGING PARTNERSHIPS, AND CREATING WIN-WIN RELATIONSHIPS PROVIDES MEANING AND COMPETITIVE ADVANTAGE.

WALK THE TALK. AS A LEADER, YOU SET THE CULTURE THROUGH YOUR WORDS, ACTIONS, AND WHAT YOU CELEBRATE. BY MODELING DESIRED BEHAVIORS, COMMUNICATING WITH TRANSPARENCY, HIRING FOR VALUES FIT, AND INSPIRING YOUR TEAM, YOU CAN REALIGN YOUR ORGANIZATION TO SUPPORT YOUR COMMUNITY-FOCUSED LEADERSHIP.

A Note to the Reader

Told through my experience and supplemented with persistent research, this book takes you on a journey. It's a voyage I believe all serious leaders must take: first, to a better understanding of themselves, then to connecting outwardly, and finally, to realigning their organization's culture, completing the integration.

This transformational trip of discovery helped me take the organizations I have served full circle, integrating their communities' values with their leadership approach.

Your journey starts when you turn the page.

Shall we begin?

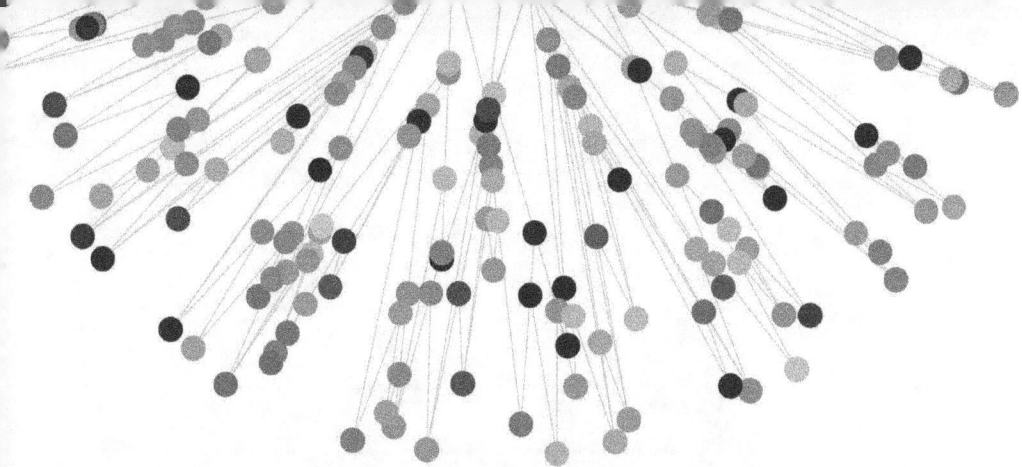

PART 1

DISCOVERING THE
LEADER WITHIN YOU

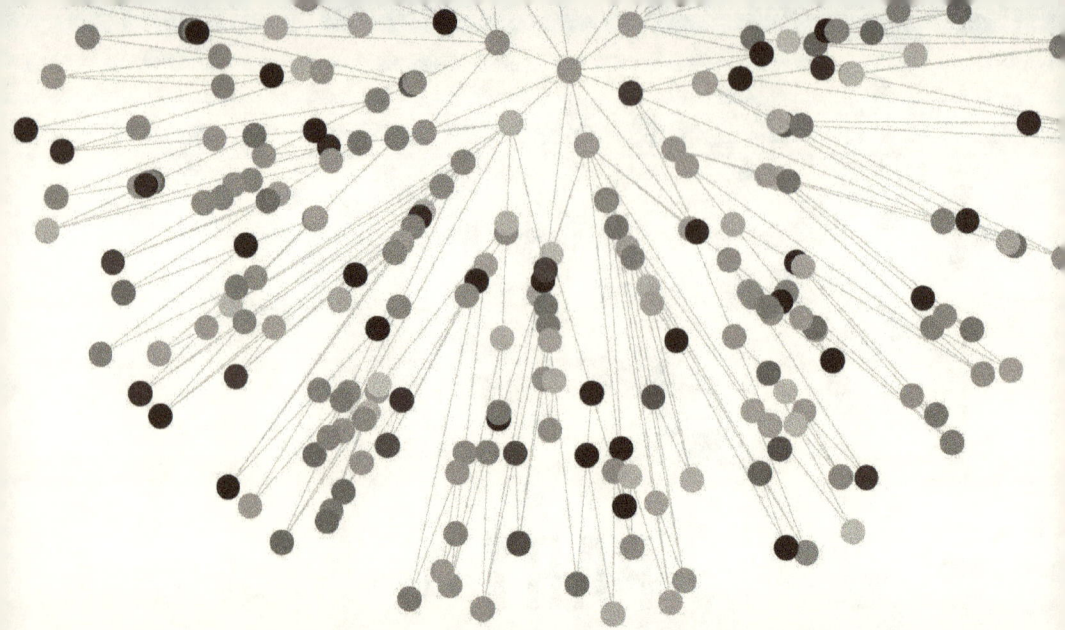

CHAPTER 1

KNOWING YOUR VALUES

If somebody offers you an amazing opportu-
nity but you are not sure you can do it, say
yes—then learn how to do it later.

—RICHARD BRANSON[5]

It was a beautiful day in late August.

Summers were always enjoyable—a quieter time in the education sector allowed more opportunities to connect with family and friends.

I was at the go-kart track with my wife and our four kids, enjoying a fun-filled adventure before another school year began. The three boys teased me because I was the slowest on the track. My four-year-old daughter even joined in the jeering.

Taking a break to watch the tiny cars making chaotic laps, I felt the flip phone's vibration in my pants pocket and opened it to answer.

---

5   Bower, T. (2014). *Branson: Behind the Mask.* Faber & Faber.

More than two decades later, I remember the conversation as if it happened yesterday.

"Enrollments in the college's guitar program are climbing," Laura, an administrator in our music department, explained. "Senior administration believes the program holds enough potential to create its first coordinator position, and we're thinking of you for the job."

At the time, I taught in the local college's music department as my "day job," but my *career* was music. Gaining notoriety on stage and in the studio as a professional guitarist was my primary focus. Teaching was simply the thing I did to pay the bills—until I was "discovered," signed a record deal, and started my world tour. Laura's appeal was a surprise opportunity I had not sought.

The sound of go-karts and the smell of gasoline were distracting. Stalling, I expressed my gratitude to Laura and agreed to meet on campus the next day to talk further.

After the call ended, my mood swung between uneasy excitement and self-doubt. Questions swirled in my mind: How would accepting this role impact my dreams? If I agreed, would coworkers support my leadership, particularly more experienced, senior colleagues? Would I have to start wearing *a tie*? Did I even *want* this role?

Five days later, I signed a one-year contract. One by one, I'd sign six more.

Across those seven years, the program's reputation grew from local to regional to national to international, with enrollment increasing by 357 percent. It happened thanks to one thing: **engagement**.

We built the organization's internal community by emphasizing staff and culture, and regularly engaged the external community— prospective students, teachers, and industry stakeholders.

But before I could engage anything or anybody, I first had to discover what leadership meant to me. So my leadership journey began. It was sparked where I now believe all successful ones are—inside ourselves.

Stage Fright

I felt unprepared for leadership; I had no training. This was over twenty years ago, and I didn't know leadership training was even "a thing." I never thought to consult books, take leadership or management courses, or seek other resources.

Instead, I went with what I knew. I led by instinct, by example, with humility, and from the heart. I worked hard; demonstrated integrity, compassion, forgiveness, and transparency; and hoped people would buy in.

Until they did, discomfort lingered. In me, as in many others who do not seek to lead, it manifested as impostor syndrome.

I was soaked with self-doubt and self-criticism, feelings I had experienced as a young music student. The same feelings I was feeling now. Back then they had manifested as stage fright, so I began thinking about how I had overcome them.

At the time I was enrolled in postsecondary music studies and played in a rock band. I practiced a lot, usually spending four to eight hours daily with a guitar in my hands. Yet in performance, my mind raced, my heart pounded, my hands shook, and nervous sweating made my leather pants uncomfortable.

After shows ended, I routinely felt frustrated and discouraged. Why couldn't I play for an audience the way I played in rehearsal? I questioned my abilities, which of course led to doubting my odds of success. Each forgettable performance convinced me that the solution must be more practice.

My guitar professor, Sharon, suggested a different remedy: redirecting some of my rehearsal time to research time. Specifically, to the study of performance psychology.

Sharon theorized that the solution to my stage fright was to become as familiar with my mindset—how I *thought* about performing—as I was with my guitar's fretboard.

Then she handed me the book that would change my life: W. Timothy Gallwey's *The Inner Game of Tennis*.[6]

Gallwey's book is a staple of sports psychology. While the title implies a deconstruction related to lined courts and merciless nets, the book's applications extend further. I instantly recognized that its techniques for improving performance were transferable to my situation. They proved to be precisely what I needed.

How could a tennis player repeatedly make a perfect drop shot on the practice court, yet float the same shot into the net in competitive play? For the very same reasons, it turns out, that a professional guitarist—in this case, me—could play flawlessly in the rehearsal room, only to struggle under his audience's gaze.

The similarities were undeniable. Like a dry sponge dropped in a pail of water, my logic soaked up the words on every page. I saw that a toxic attitude toward performance was inhibiting my ability to play onstage with the intuitive abandon I brought to rehearsal.

Put simply, Gallwey's "inner game" is one we all play, against our own minds. In other words, *we're* our own worst opponents.

The book led to my embrace of performance psychology. It introduced me to my "Self 1" (the teller) and "Self 2" (the doer): respectively, my conscious and unconscious minds. It showed how tangible success required *mental* practice, a commitment to quieting

---

6   Gallwey, W. T. (1974). *The inner game of tennis: The classic guide to the mental side of peak performance.* Random House.

Self 1—my toxic, internal critic—so I could perform with an uncluttered, nonjudgmental mind.

At the same time, I trained Self 2—my intuition, the sum of my experience and practice—to play a more prominent, positive mental role and, by so doing, to drive my performance.

The results were transformational. I began to find success, but more importantly, I felt *at home* on the concert stage.

Gallwey's book pushed me outside of my comfort zone. It had never occurred to me that I could become a better performer, a decidedly outward-facing objective, by looking *inward*, without even holding my "axe."

The Inner Game of Leadership

After agreeing to coordinate the college's guitar program, one of my fears vanished immediately: my colleagues, it turned out, were encouraging and supportive.

Still, as I tried to settle in, my Self 1 was back at it, cluttering my thoughts with judgmental noise and self-criticism. Impostor syndrome was back.

I returned to my worn copy of *The Inner Game,* determined this time to apply its principles to my new leadership career. Sure enough, the tools helped quiet Self 1 and allowed Self 2 to trust my preparation and instincts.

Coming back to Gallwey's book and seeing the results solidified my commitment to reading to spark my development as a leader. And not just in becoming the leader my constituents deserved, but the leader *I wanted* to be.

Diving into a sea of writings, I found a favorite in Dale Carnegie's timeless *How to Win Friends and Influence People*.[7] The applicability of its charming lessons, almost a century after the book's publication, increased my determination to foster my growth as a leader.

As its title suggests, executive coach Kelsey Meyer's *Why Leaders Must Be Readers* highlights the need to read for volume in building knowledge and to review favorite writings to keep essential concepts top of mind.[8] Each book that spoke to me further quieted my self-criticism and inner doubt.

Author and coach Tony Robbins writes that success leaves clues and encourages leaders to study success at all levels and across all sectors.[9] So beyond leadership theory, I studied the lives of effective leaders: champions in business, politics, sports, and the arts.

Each of these volumes imparted valuable lessons. The process reminded me of music school, where I learned how Mozart studied the string quartets of Haydn; Mendelssohn saw the genius in J. S. Bach;[10] Keith Richards "wore out" his recordings of Chuck Berry; Jimi Hendrix took inspiration from Bob Dylan; and Eddie Van Halen was "touched" by the work of Eric Clapton.[11]

In short, I became the poster child for Hermina Ibarra's words. A professor of organizational behavior at the London Business School,

---

7   Carnegie, D. (1936). *How to Win Friends and Influence People.* Simon & Schuster.

8   Meyer, K. (2012). Why leaders must be readers. *Forbes.* Retrieved from https://www.forbes.com/sites/85broads/2012/08/03/why-leaders-must-be-readers/?sh=7bf9ccc94736

9   Robbins, T. (2020). Business Mastery, live event.

10   Burkholder, J. P., Grout, D. J., & Palisca, C. V. (2019). *A history of Western music: Tenth international student edition.* W. W. Norton & Company.

11   Various. (1995). *History of rock 'n' roll.* 10 Part TV Series. Retrieved from https://www.imdb.com/title/tt5278426/

she writes that impostor syndrome, or "feeling like a fake," can lead to growth—*by inspiring learning.*[12]

My learnings consistently emphasized self-awareness, defining it as a leader's greatest tool. I developed my own by studying emotional intelligence—or as Korn Ferry, the global organizational consultancy, calls it, *emotional* self-awareness.[13]

Organizational psychologist Tasha Eurich defines self-awareness as having two broad categories: internal and external.[14] Parts 2 and 3 of this book will discuss external self-awareness—understanding how *other* people see *us.* Here in part 1, we'll look at the internal variety, which leads to a fuller understanding of ourselves.

The Necessity of Looking Inside

Emotional quotient (EQ) is the ability to understand and manage our emotions in order to access them as essential leadership tools. One of its pioneers is Daniel Goleman, of whom I am a shameless fanboy. Goleman's work encompasses the wider field of emotional intelligence (EI)[15] as well. I highly recommend all his writings but will return to the concept and use of one's EQ throughout this book.

Goleman explains that understanding EI unlocks critical skills like self-awareness, self-regulation, motivation, and empathy.[16] His

---

12   Ibarra, H. (2015). The authenticity paradox. *Harvard Business Review, 93*(1/2), 53–59.

13   Ferry, K. (2024). Mindful leadership: The importance of self-awareness. Retrieved from https://www.kornferry.com/insights/featured-topics/leadership/ mindful-leadership-the-importance-of-self-awareness

14   Eurich, T. (2018). What self-awareness really is (and how to cultivate it). *Harvard Business Review, 4.*

15   Goleman, D. (1995). *Emotional intelligence: Why it can matter more than IQ.* Bantam.

16   Goleman, D., Boyatzis, R., and McKee, A. (2013). *Primal leadership: Unleashing the power of emotional intelligence.* Harvard Business Review Press.

work led me to realize that EQ is a measurable skill that can be continually developed and improved.

Working to enhance my EQ has significantly impacted my leadership skills. I now strive to be consistently aware of my emotional state. Whether reading an email, talking on the phone, or meeting in the board room, I've learned to ensure that my "EQ radar" is always on and evaluate my *emotional* state, as surely as my nervous system monitors changes to my physical one.

My EQ radar now alerts me when my emotions change, whether due to a particular situation, something I've read, or things I've heard. It's taken years, but I've trained myself to become conscious of every change that signals an emotional response, from body temperature rising to my mind "racing" and hijacking my thoughts.

Early in my leadership career, the mere "turning on" of my EQ radar had an immediate effect. Where heightened emotional states had once led me to act, I began to proceed with thoughtful caution instead: to pause, to breathe, to be curious.

It was the same path I'd taken in conquering stage fright: just before I went onstage, my hands would become cold, my heart would race, my thinking would accelerate—sometimes, I'd begin to pray that a power failure would cancel the show!

But as I worked on my inner (guitar) game, I learned to recognize and acknowledge these signals. Gradually, instead of judging myself or trying to push such feelings down, I accepted them, learned about them, and—by understanding them—overcame them.

I brought the same approach to my leadership journey, observing and listening to what was happening for me without judgment, no matter how frustrating or absurd my feelings might have seemed. Over time, my EQ radar became my most trusted tool. It showed me the power of mindset, of looking inward, and of working on one's self first.

But a closer knowledge of my emotional status was only the start. My inner journey of leadership also required me to take a hard look at my values.

Values-Based Leadership: The High Ground

As children, our values typically align with those of our family. As we grow, our circle of influence does too. School, church, work, and hobbies introduce us to people and experiences that inform our values.

My first leadership role (born of that phone call at the go-kart track) helped affirm my belief in the value of community and led me to identify another key value: **personal growth**. Knowing and upholding these values has since allowed me to lead organizations that became beacons in their respective communities, fostering employee growth, internal culture, and external engagement.

James Kouzes and Barry Posner, authors of *The Leadership Challenge*,[17] write that the better we understand who we are and what we believe in, the better we make sense of the often incomprehensible and conflicting demands we receive as leaders.[18] Despite the numerous choices and opinions we confront daily, by making decisions rooted in our values, we will always find ourselves on high ground.

But how do we *get* to that high ground?

---

17   Kouzes, J. M., & Posner, B. Z. (2006). *The leadership challenge* (Vol. 3). John Wiley & Sons.

18   Ibid.

In the climactic scene of George Lucas's epic *Star Wars: Revenge of the Sith*, Anakin Skywalker battles his mentor, Obi-Wan Kenobi.[19] It's a classic duel between apprentice and master.

In the battle, Anakin gives in to emotions that feed the dark side of the Force: fear, anger, and aggression. But Obi-Wan remains true to his Jedi values throughout and wins the high ground, morally but also literally. Despite Obi-Wan's compassionate warning, Anakin makes a desperate upward leap, and Obi-Wan's lightsaber inflicts life-changing wounds that accelerate Anakin's transformation to Darth Vader.

Trey Taylor, another of my favorite thinkers, has a way of simplifying what seems to be the complicated topic of leadership. We can only hope to understand and lead others, he writes, once we understand ourselves.[20]

Knowing and being true to ourselves: *That's* how we get to the high ground.

Leaders are regularly questioned, even challenged. Kouzes and Posner write that leaders must first take an inner journey, discovering who we are and what we care about, because success—in business and in life—depends on how well we know ourselves, what we value, and why we value it.[21] This inner journey requires alone time, with a commitment to honest, thoughtful reflection.

Looking Inward

Finding that time can be a tricky thing for leaders. Countless people will want to connect with you, whether in person, via email, phone,

---

19   Lucas, G. (2005). *Star wars: Episode III—revenge of the Sith*. 20th Century Fox.

20   Taylor, T. (2020). *A CEO only does three things*. Board Advisors.

21   Kouzes, J. M., & Posner, B. Z. (2011). Leadership begins with an inner journey. *Leader to Leader, 2011*(60), 22–27.

text, video call, or through social media. How are we supposed to find time for thoughtful reflection?

By *making* the time.

Let's say you are determined to improve your physical fitness. Perhaps you run, swim, bike, visit the gym, or walk during your lunch hour. You do it because it is important to you. For the same reason, leaders must set time aside to work their "leadership muscles." For me, only one thing has worked: scheduling it.

In *The Inner Game of Tennis*, chief among W. Timothy Gallwey's teachings is experimenting and discovering what works for you.[22] My mind is clearest early in the day when outside noise and chatter are quietest.

(Author's note: Throughout this book I have changed the names of the institutions I served, and the identities and personal details of those I've worked with, in order to clearly explain situations I have faced without disparaging the individuals who were involved.)

Today, as president and CEO at what I'll call Grasslands College, I arrive at work early each morning. Only the custodians and security guards are on campus. The quiet calm is almost surreal compared to what I know is coming later in the day.

While I sit alone in my office, slowly sipping the day's first coffee, I create what has proved, for me, to be the perfect environment for reflection. I engage my self-awareness and consider what kind of leader I am, what kind of leader I want to be, how I can better serve my organization, and how these realities and aspirations might manifest into tangible values that can guide my decisions. With my journal close by, I allow my experiences, interactions, and conversations to bubble up. I especially contemplate the behaviors I've observed in myself to help me more fully identify my values.

---

22 Gallwey, T. (1974).

Sometimes I surprise myself. Trey Taylor says our values may be conscious, unconscious, or somewhere in between—and may even be aspirational.[23] Experience has confirmed for me that profound insight can spring up when we least expect it, and that's just what happened one Saturday afternoon.

I was sitting at a restaurant patio, having arrived earlier than the rest of my party (as usual). While waiting, I engaged my waitress, Janna, in conversation. She noticed my T-shirt, which featured a large logo of the university where I worked and became quite animated. She was a current student, she said, and asked if I was a professor.

"I'm an administrator," I said. "A dean." She seemed disappointed.

"I'm a nursing student," Janna said.

"Wow, that's tough to get into," I said. "Congratulations!" Our nursing program featured the university's most competitive acceptance process.

Janna explained that before entering the program, she was enrolled in academic upgrading, which helps students improve their previous high school grades and prepares them for the demands of a postsecondary curriculum. I told Janna that academic upgrading was in my portfolio—I used to be her dean!

Her excitement returned, but she became more serious.

Janna explained that her life had presented many challenges and that success at school had once seemed impossible. She owned making some poor choices in the past but described how impactful "my" upgrading program had been. She shared that the support of the staff and professors had given her a second chance.

She was grateful—and there, just as Trey Taylor promised, was my profound, totally unexpected insight: *our work was helping change people's lives.*

---

23 Taylor, T. (2020).

Experiences like this one—and cultivating the habit of reflecting on them—have helped define my "why," the reason I do what I do. Janna was every student I wanted to serve, and that day, I discovered firsthand why access—access to education for all who seek a better future—is one of my core values.

Reflection helped me better understand myself as a leader. That knowledge, in turn, led me to the next step: discovering how my values aligned with those of my employer.

Values-Based Leadership

Years after my chat with Janna, I held a leadership role at an institution that had recently completed its strategic planning process. I contributed to the focus groups that guided the process and spent plenty of one-on-one time with the university's contracted facilitators.

Yet when the consultants unveiled their plan to senior leadership, I felt confused and discouraged. I did not see my core beliefs reflected in the school's mission, in its vision, nor, most distressingly, in its values.

The blunt realization that my values did not align with my employer's was overwhelming. How could I be a successful ambassador—let alone a senior leader—for an organization I was this poorly aligned with?

Thankfully, I enjoyed a good working relationship with the university's leader. I went to President Tom and respectfully conveyed my dilemma.

In his patient, thoughtful response, he encouraged me to imagine putting the newly minted strategic plan into a sifter, like those miners used during the Klondike Gold Rush.

"Give the sifter a good shake and see what falls out to the ground. And then," he added, "take those nuggets and embrace them."

President Tom was telling me that I didn't need to see myself in *all* the plan, only some of it. Thanking him, I decided to take his advice back to my early morning reflection sessions.

I gave the document plenty of time and consideration but still struggled to connect with its values. Most conspicuous for its absence, given its importance to me, was access. Once a hallmark of the institution's reputation, access was no longer an organizational value, though I searched for it among those "nuggets that fell to the ground."

I immediately knew that my professional journey was at a crossroads.

The Crossroads

Bluesman Robert Johnson remains a fascinating figure. His legend includes the tale of trading his soul to the devil at the crossroads in exchange for musical success.[24] Johnson perpetuated this claim through his songs, including "Crossroad Blues," "Me and the Devil Blues," and "Hellhounds on My Trail."[25]

I sat in my office reflecting. It was unfair to compare my employer to Satan—I felt appreciated and fairly compensated. But was this the deal I *wanted*? My values did not align with the organization's values. I could stay and just keep cashing the checks, but could I live with myself if I did? Could I exchange my values—*my soul*—for success?

---

24   Guralnick, P. (1998). *Searching for Robert Johnson: The life and legend of the King of the Delta Blues Singers*. Plume Books.

25   Wald, E. (2004). *Escaping the delta: Robert Johnson and the invention of the blues*. Amistad Press.

President Tom's sifting exercise prompted my discovery of another core value: **authenticity**. And just like that, I knew: it was time to start looking for a new job.

I had to leave because my heart told me that I couldn't sell something I didn't believe in. Despite my background in performance, this was no act. I wanted to stand before my constituents and speak with honesty and passion. I wanted—needed—to uphold my values.

A year later I was at a new institution, with a new opportunity: to practice, each day, values that aligned more closely with my own.

> VALUES-BASED LEADERSHIP GOES BEYOND THE BOTTOM LINE TO CREATE AUTHENTIC BUY-IN.

Values-based leadership goes beyond the bottom line to create authentic buy-in.

Mark Carney's impressive résumé includes stints as governor of the banks of England and of Canada, along with other A-list gigs. He writes that values-based leaders generate enthusiastic engagement among colleagues and other stakeholders, including the consent of their community to operate.[26] This fosters organizational success by activating community engagement and nurturing corporate culture—both of which are at the core of this book's premise.

Closing Thoughts

Few are trained for leadership. Like many, I was offered the mantle of leadership because of the job I'd done on the front lines.

When thrown into roles for which we are unprepared, we have two options. We can allow fear (or stage fright) to limit us, or we can approach it as a journey, complete with detours and, often, surprising new routes.

---

26   Carney, M. (2023). *Value(s): Building a better world for all*. Penguin Random House.

Though my success brought more opportunities, and my leadership roles compounded naturally, I questioned my qualifications for holding every last one of them. By taking the second approach, I learned that impostor syndrome is common and that being a leader is an inner game—just as overcoming stage fright had been years before. Quieting the internal chatter that fed my doubts gave me faith in my abilities and confidence in my intuition.

That work is never complete. Like an athlete training in the gym, I continue to train my mental muscles and to monitor their status with my EQ radar. Reflection helps me identify my values and intentionally live by them. Quiet time each morning illuminates insights from past conversations and experiences and allows me to anticipate future scenarios and consider strategies for managing them. That daily practice ensures that my values come through in my interactions and decision-making.

To me, that is the definition of authentic leadership.

Key Takeaways

This chapter explored leadership's personal journey of discovering core values and purpose.

- A leader must be able to share their values: what they are and why they matter to them.

- Reflection fuels development. Schedule time for reflection and consider keeping a journal.

- Know your place. Understand if, and how, your values align with those of your organization.

For Reflection

- What are *your* core values? (There are no wrong answers. Your values are yours.)

- What experiences shaped your values? (Knowing this will be helpful in the next two chapters.)

- Remember a time that you lived your leadership values.

- Think back to a situation that challenged or compromised your values.

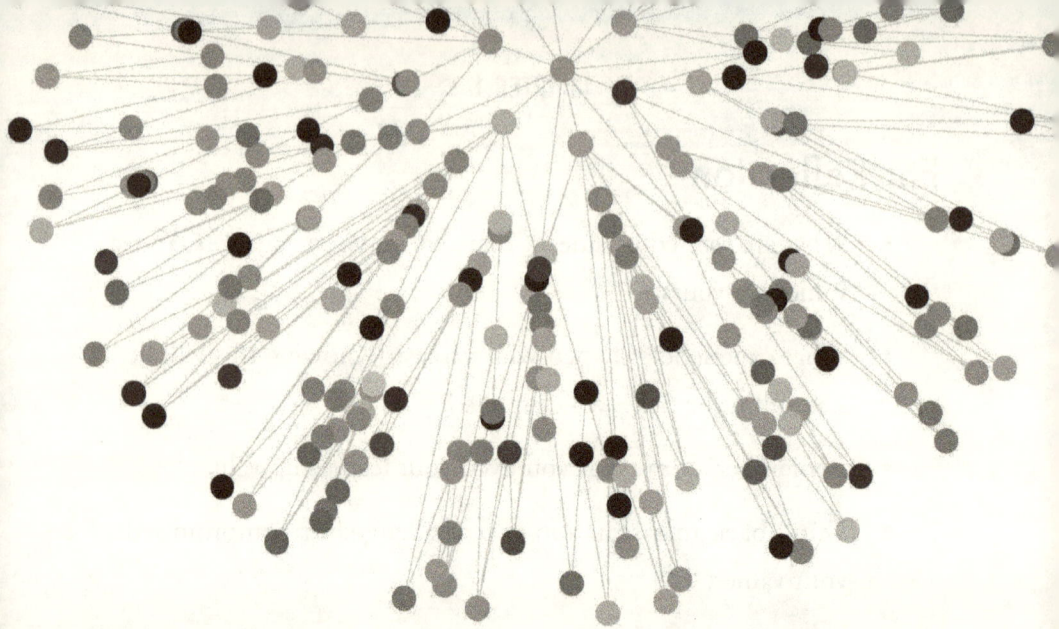

CHAPTER 2

FINDING YOUR VOICE

Find your voice and inspire others to find theirs.

—STEPHEN COVEY[27]

The young daughter and three sons who mocked my go-kart skills at the opening of this book were a decade older now. I had recently accepted the role of director at what, for reasons I'll soon make clear, I'll call Protest University, overseeing the institution's conservatory of music, with 20 administrative staff, 150 instructors, and about 4,500 students.

On my first day, the dean smiled and firmly shook my hand.

"Everything is set for you to implement your vision. Difficult decisions have been made. The winds of change have blown. We've cleared the path for you. The heavy lifting is done."

---

27   Covey, S. R. (2020). *The 7 habits of highly effective people*. Simon & Schuster.

I felt uneasy—and not just because of my new boss's overuse of metaphors. All was not well at Protest U. I'd learned of the troubles several months before during the recruitment process.

Finances were problematic. Programs and people had been cut. On the day of my job interview, students, faculty, staff, and donors protested on the concert hall's front steps, unified in anger.

The unrest attracted significant media attention, complete with stories of unhappiness over recent decisions by senior leadership. Following these happenings from afar, living in another city while the interview process proceeded, was surreal.

It quickly got real once I'd accepted the job, and a basic, practical question surfaced, spawned from a previous experience: Where would I park my car?

At another school, I'd overseen precollege performing arts programs, and the competitive dance program was struggling. Students' parents were especially vocal. As I made hard decisions, difficult conversations followed, but at my own insistence; I considered honest interaction fundamental to another of my core leadership values: **transparency**.

So my door was open, offering an ear and forthright conversation to anyone requesting them. Still, it got weird. Parents started waiting for me in the parking lot, because my personalized license plate made my car easy to find: "DRGUITR."

Their relentless presence persuaded me to park on the opposite end of campus. I wondered if doing so might be prudent at Protest U.

The situation, however, was a bit different. There was truth in some of the dean's encouraging words. Difficult decisions *had* been made, so my charge was to fulfill the rationale behind them. Yet the path was far from clear, and *plenty* of heavy lifting waited in the wings.

Is This Mic Working?

There were parallels between this situation and my performing career.

Onstage, though I had learned to control my nerves, there were still awkward moments.

I'd played thousands of shows with guitar in hand but had rarely sung—it's not why people hire me. But I still had a mic and used it to communicate with the audience.

When it failed and that connection was lost, I was unnerved—and that's just how I felt in this new role: struggling to find my voice in order to communicate my values and vision.

When I spoke, people didn't listen. *They* wanted to do the talking. They didn't want to hear about new program ideas or expanded partnerships. They were waiting for *me* to fall silent, so *they* could speak.

I had succeeded at fostering organizational culture and cultivating external engagement and collaboration in the past. Yet at Protest U, I found a disengaged community and a disgruntled staff. Partnerships had ended, staff had left or been dismissed, students had transferred, and donor support had shrunk. People were hurt, and that negative impact lingered.

They shared their expectations and opinions on what my focus should be. Staff hoped I would undo decisions or, as they saw it, "right the wrongs." Superiors wanted me to calm the waves by bringing a new vision to the organization that would end the protests.

Opposing advice flowed from every rung of the organizational ladder, and each day, I became more reactive—the antithesis of my normally proactive approach. Noise was everywhere.

How could I remedy the fact that people just weren't interested in what I had to say?

Perhaps a new role required a new approach—an alternate leadership style?

The Change Room: Trying on Other Styles

I feel fortunate to have experienced the full range of leadership styles: energetic leaders who inspired all via their contagious passion, accessible leaders who walked the hallways and whose doors were always open, communicative leaders who kept employees updated, and dedicated leaders who worked tirelessly.

Then there were those who rarely shared information, seemed disinterested, or were "invisible"—whose employees admitted they couldn't pick their leader out in a police lineup. Finally, there were leaders who leveraged fear, flexed their muscles, and strictly enforced a hierarchical, or top-down, style.

As a bottom-up guy, I find leaders' use of fear to be particularly fascinating.

Dr. Margie Warrell, a *Forbes* writer and international speaker on human potential, writes that while leading by punishing candor and rewarding compliance may yield results, its negative long-term effects on employee performance and morale are notable too.[28]

I once had a direct supervisor who terrified me, and I was not alone.

Consulting with his other direct reports, we discovered that each of us had broken down after meetings and felt like we were failing as leaders. But the relationship was complex: we had to grudgingly acknowledge that his truthful feedback also motivated us. We were

---

28   Warrell, M. (2023). *Leaders who manage by fear make everyone less secure.* Forbes. Retrieved from https://www.forbes.com/sites/margiewarrell/2023/02/15/ leaders-who-manage-by-fear-make-everyone-less-secure/?sh=4e50f6a5543e

determined to learn, take lessons away, and find value in the difficult encounters. We also knew we'd be better leaders for it.

Not everyone responds so positively to an authoritative leadership style. I understand this today, but learned it the hard way as I struggled to settle into my new director's role at Protest U.

Though a few months had passed since I'd joined the school, the challenges lingered, and I was, frankly, about fed up with them. While many stakeholders were unhappy with more recent events and decisions, it was becoming clear that some had *never* been happy and likely never would be. Several of these folks saw my status as their new leader as a chance to air historical grievances.

Dan, a longtime employee, was one of those people. When he requested a meeting, I asked two of my staff to join us. I also brought to the session a frustration-fueled determination to bring some immediate order to the ongoing chaos—and to do it by *sending a message*.

What a disaster.

With an air of what felt to me like self-assurance built on a sense of entitlement, given his long tenure at Protest U, Dan outlined his grievances and ideal outcomes.

As he spoke, my EQ radar sprung to life. I sensed changes in my physiology. A wave of heat overtook me. My mind raced. Anger brewed. Months of frustration were about to boil over.

Like a lion stalking its prey, my eyes locked on Dan.

I met his address with a counterattack—blasting his case. My voice was aggressive, and I quickly set him up for the knockout. "It is clear to me, Dan, that the organization can't give you what you want, and vice versa." I let the words hang in the air momentarily, then threw my haymaker.

"I think it's time for a change, for both parties."

Dan's assuredness vanished. He seemed surprised, even wounded. The two employees who had joined the meeting were silent and noticeably uncomfortable. The meeting reached an awkward end as quickly as it had begun, and the three attendees departed my office.

I sat alone for several minutes, with everything feeling wrong, a feeling that soon persuaded me to check on my two staff members.

I approached a closed office door and softly knocked. My colleague opened it and invited me in. She had been crying.

"Why the emotions?" I asked.

"I've never heard you talk to someone that way," she replied.

Physiologic manifestations of discomfort again washed over me. My stomach hurt. My mind raced. I didn't know how to respond. I quietly apologized and left her office, closing the door behind me.

Later that day, I received Dan's resignation letter.

I had found *a* voice—but was it *my voice*? It couldn't be. It felt terrible.

More than a decade later, I still reflect on that meeting and likely always will.

In attempting to understand what had transpired, I first tried to justify the voice I had chosen to use that day.

I was a leader whose door was always open, I reasoned. I walked the halls. I welcomed discussions with anyone—about anything. Yet in this new role, the drama had exhausted me, and I'd decided to send a message to everyone that I could only be pushed so far.

They had pushed me to this result. This was on *them*. It was *their* fault.

I tried to convince myself that my voice *didn't require* an explanation. I was the *boss*. I flexed. I dropped the hammer. I fired a warning shot. (Apparently, the dean's love of metaphors was affecting me.)

It didn't work.

When I looked inward, I couldn't convince myself that this was who I was, let alone the leader I wanted to be.

That doesn't mean the decision to move on from this employee was wrong. Even today, I know it was the best thing for the organization.

But there was a better way to handle the situation.

At length, I admitted to myself that I had acted poorly. Then I went further, questioning whether leadership was really for me.

I recognized that I had used a voice—and shown a style of leadership—that only *reinforced* the root cause of the campus turmoil: hierarchical, authoritative, top-down, compassionless, and void of self-awareness. I had employed *fear*, the very emotion that had *prompted* our stakeholders' rebellion.

But wait. It gets worse. Word of the incident with Dan spread.

How would I rebuild trust so we could all move forward together?

I again looked inward and returned to my values—notably, personal growth. I promised myself that I would always remember that meeting, my voice, my behavior, and the terrible feelings it created for all involved. Ultimately, I committed fully to learning from the experience and becoming a better leader because of it.

I had given myself the same grace that I'd allowed the authoritarian leader under whom I'd worked earlier in my career: I didn't like the approach, but if that turned out to be the big takeaway from the experience, it had still taught me something of value.

This made me feel a little better, yet in that place and at that moment, I was still overcome with a sense of urgency.

I needed to find my *authentic* voice—and fast.

Finding Your Voice by Listening

Over my career as a professional guitarist, I have collaborated with incredible musicians and played masterpieces spanning the centuries, from Mozart to Hendrix.

The technical demands of such works require me to "keep up my chops" by maintaining a daily practice schedule and doing live performances to keep my inner game sharp. Still, there's a tool that has proved more essential to my development as a musician than practice or performance: my ears.

As the turmoil I'd inherited at Protest U continued, it became clear that I'd need to bring that tool—my ability to *listen*—to my leadership journey.

It's understandable, I guess, for leaders to think that everyone wants to hear and know their vision. I certainly thought so. Yet the more I *listened,* the clearer it became that what stakeholders want most is to *be heard.*

Seizing the urgency I felt to make things better, I set up one-on-one meetings with every employee and genuinely listened, methodically hearing and assimilating all they said.

AS THEY SPOKE, I FOCUSED ON THEIR WORDS.

I LISTENED TO *HEAR* RATHER THAN PREPARING MY REPLY.

I PLAYED THE INNER GAME, BANISHING JUDGMENTAL THOUGHTS FROM MY MIND.

I MAINTAINED EYE CONTACT, SOMETIMES NODDING TO SIGNAL MY CONTINUED ENGAGEMENT.

I TOOK NOTES—BUT NOT TOO MANY, IN ORDER TO MAINTAIN OUR VISUAL CONNECTION.

ABOVE ALL ELSE, I REMEMBERED THAT THIS PERSON WAS MY *COLLEAGUE.*

When each had finished talking, I paused and reflected on their words. Next, I thoughtfully reframed what I'd heard, checking to be sure I fully understood the depth and breadth of their input.

I didn't try to solve anything in the moment, but instead promised to think about what I had heard and to follow up. And I concluded *every session* by expressing my gratitude for the learning opportunity this person had provided me.

Make no mistake: these conversations were difficult, even emotional—to the point that a Kleenex box came to reside on my conference table (and an antacid product lurked in my desk drawer).

As I made good on my promise of follow-up conversations, connections with my coworkers gradually strengthened.

Soon, I organized a meeting with the full staff.

I recounted the overarching themes I'd heard during the one-on-ones, shared the values I'd identified, and revealed my own, highlighting where we had alignment. I gratefully and genuinely acknowledged to the entire group the new perspectives I'd gained.

As I spoke, I felt their eyes locked on mine, their heads nodding, their thoughtful attention. I had listened to them, and now—at last—they were listening to me.

The meeting ended, and the staff slowly exited. Each had a brief exchange with me as they departed—sometimes a handshake, other times a nod and smile. Sometimes, our eyes would lock, and I would hear a quiet "Thank you."

Others gathered in small groups in the room's corners, debriefing softly among themselves. My EQ radar read the atmosphere: it was tranquil, a quality that had been in scarce supply in this new place, until now.

As the acclaimed author Stephen Covey writes, leaders must seek *first* to understand, *then* to be understood.[29]

This time, I'd found my *authentic* voice—the voice of the leader I wanted to be.

Through reflection and self-awareness, my voice manifested my values—most notably, empathy. I continue this process of understanding myself as a leader to this day, because knowing my strengths and identifying my blind spots are equally crucial to becoming the leader my constituents deserve.

Feedback: Understanding Our Strengths and Gaps

Feedback is a gift, but by the time it reaches leadership, it can be sugar-coated at best, downright fabricated at worst. This is not a criticism of our employees; it is a reality of our hierarchical world.

Carolyn Dewar, Scott Keller, and Vikram Malhotra, authors of *CEO Excellence*, acknowledge the difficulty faced by leaders, especially senior leaders, in receiving honest feedback.[30] After all, who wants to tell the boss that their "state of the union" speech fell flat?

---

29   Covey, S. R. (2020). *The 7 habits of highly effective people.* Simon & Schuster.

30   Dewar, C., Keller, S., & Malhotra, V. (2022). *CEO excellence: The six mindsets that distinguish the best leaders from the rest.* Simon & Schuster.

But what's a leader to do? Let's revisit a topic from chapter 1: self-awareness.

I cited Tasha Eurich, an organizational psychologist, who defines self-awareness as having two broad categories: internal and external.[31] While managing our internal reactions is critical, developing external self-awareness to understand how people see us can help us learn our strengths and discover our blind spots. It was through this process that I identified one of my gaps.

Working with Frank, a campus manager, was exhausting. After a year of coaching and crucial conversations, he still struggled to accept my changes and embrace our new organizational direction. I decided it was time for a change.

These are always difficult decisions, but this one was especially hard because I liked Frank personally. I invited him to my office, where I informed him of my decision.

As we concluded, he asked if he'd be "walked out." I respected Frank and wanted to show he still had my trust, so I assured him he would not be. Instead, I suggested that he take the next two days to summarize the state of his portfolio and have concluding conversations with colleagues as he saw fit. I told him I trusted that he would respect me and the organization in those chats and in his actions and promised to send him a draft of the staffing announcement for his feedback the next day, before it was posted.

He—we—had agreed to navigate his departure collaboratively.

Frank seemed relieved and expressed his appreciation. We shook hands, and I felt like we were on the high ground. Why couldn't all employment relationships end in such a harmonious way? *Maybe I should write a book*, I thought.

---

31   Eurich, T. (2018). What self-awareness really is (and how to cultivate it). *Harvard Business Review, 4.*

Not so fast, Brad.

Frank's all-staff email hit inboxes the next morning.

My stomach turned. This was not what Frank and I had agreed to. The message was derogatory in tone and critical of my decision and of my overall leadership.

However, I wasn't angry with Frank. I was disappointed in *myself*.

I had let personal feelings affect my professional judgment. Reflection and self-awareness provided feedback and revealed a blind spot.

I took a lesson from the experience, but I also appreciated the organizational intelligence, which confirmed that Frank's damage was minimal.

I respectfully refer to the staff who provided that intel as …

SPIES

That's right, *spies*.

Sun Tzu's *The Art of War* has tutored leaders for centuries. I knew of the book but had passed on it because its title struck me as extreme. Yet as my leadership posts advanced and scenarios intensified, I realized it might offer insight.

Today, I own four different editions.

I transferred Tzu's military references as I read, adapting his metaphors into valuable leadership advice. I was especially struck by his discussion of the importance of spies, which he calls "a ruler's treasures."[32] Among the gifts these "treasures" bring is feedback. It reminded me of a time early in my first tenure as a president.

From the moment I met Vince, it was clear: this wasn't going to work.

Vince was one of my vice presidents. He was also my opposite: authoritarian, hierarchical, and indifferent to company culture, to the

---

32   Tzu, S. (1994). *The art of war*. Basic Books.

client experience, to community engagement. And socially awkward to boot.

Still, I valued having different people at my leadership table, with diverse ways of thinking and dissimilar approaches. I knew the company would be doomed if I created an executive table only of "Brads."

Still, the evidence against Vince mounted.

It was bad enough that his portfolio was struggling, but most alarming was his seeming indifference to the company's success. It became a matter of when, not if, I would make the change. But timing mattered: Moving too early in my tenure might make me look impulsive, as if I hadn't taken time to fully learn about the organization. Waiting too long might make me appear indecisive.

We finally parted ways with Vince respectfully, ensuring he was set up well for whatever the next chapter in his professional journey might be. It was my first big move at the executive table.

And sure enough, my "treasures" weighed in on my performance.

Like a scene from a spy movie, I met my first informant in his basement office.

He told me my decision was well received by the staff, though some questioned the timing—wondering why I'd taken so *long*. A second spy affirmed this. In fact, he said, it seemed that if I had taken any longer, I might have lost popular support.

It was intelligence *gold*.

Reflecting on the feedback, I tried, just as I had with my clumsy dismissal of Dan years before, to justify my actions. It's what we humans do. I told myself I had delayed because it was an important decision—someone's career.

But I knew they were right. I had waited too long.

Dewar, Keller, and Malhotra, whose acknowledgment of the importance of feedback I referenced earlier in this chapter, consider decisiveness a key trait for successful leadership.[33] Though I instinctively knew from our first meeting that VP Vince had to go, I had been hesitant to trust my intuition.

Francesca Sipma, founder and CEO of Mastry, considers intuition a superpower in business—that voice inside us that comes from a deep sense of knowing and cannot be accessed from our logical or analytical mind.[34]

Meanwhile, in *Forbes,* Sean O'Neal has written that intuition is the richest source of wisdom because it is built on past experience, uniquely bridging the intellectual response of analysis with the emotional reaction of instinct.[35]

Self-awareness (and spies!) can help cultivate meaningful feedback, which reveals both strengths and gaps. Yet feedback can also come from inside ourselves. My handling of Vince's dismissal alerted me to indecisiveness but, at the same time, affirmed intuition as a strength.

Silent Signs

I learned to watch for other feedback forms during that first lonely year as a president.

I was driving to work one winter morning, totally "in my head."

It had been a rough few days. Six months into my tenure, it felt like I was losing my inner game. I judged myself and asked hard

33 Dewar, C., Keller, S., & Malhotra, V. (2022). *CEO excellence: The six mindsets that distinguish the best leaders from the rest.* Simon & Schuster.

34 Sipma, F. (2022). *Why intuition is a superpower in business.* Forbes. Retrieved from https://www.forbes.com/sites/forbesbusinesscouncil/2022/06/22/why-intuition-is-a-superpower-in-business/?sh=7fe16dfd3539

35 O'Neal, S. (2021). *In business, don't rely on instinct: Why intuition is different and better.* Forbes. Retrieved from https://www.forbes.com/sites/forbesbusinesscouncil/2021/05/04/in-business-dont-rely-on-instinct-why-intuition-is-different-and-better/?sh=6faa744231fe

questions: Was I making a difference? Was the organization in a better place? *Should I even go to work today?*

As I neared the campus, I noted the perfectly blanketed parking lot—uniformly white from the prior night's snowfall. It was early; there wasn't a car in the lot. Snow crunched under my wheels as I approached my assigned parking stall. I slowed the car and strained my eyes to confirm what I saw.

The stall had been cleared of snow, and a footpath cleared from my stall to the building.

It was the only snow that had been cleared among the hundreds of stalls. I stopped my vehicle where it was and gazed at the lone piece of clear asphalt and the connecting pathway. Then I stepped outside and took a few photos to capture the moment.

The custodians had given me informal positive feedback before. As my first fall term progressed and the prairie mornings grew colder, I entered my office early one morning to find my space heater turned on.

It started happening daily, and when I mentioned it to others in the executive suite, they reacted with surprise and raised eyebrows. It seems this was unprecedented.

I appreciated the warm office that awaited my morning reflections as a form of feedback.

Sometimes, the best feedback a leader gets—good and bad—is unspoken.

Risk-Reward

Early in my leadership career, my developing voice consistently had a tone of optimistic positivity and was delivered with enthusiastic energy. Some associated it with my newness and naivete—my lack of years in the leadership trenches had not yet, they reasoned, beaten me down.

Twenty-plus years on, I have continued to use that voice of optimism and worked to maintain its enthusiasm. Like the dual lessons I took from how I'd severed the relationship with Frank, I wondered if my optimism—manifested in faith and trust—might be a blind spot too.

Remember President Tom from chapter 1? As I prepared to leave his organization for my first presidency role, he generously spent time with me, lent me books, and debriefed me on their lessons.

In the years since, we'd often discussed leadership topics. I could count on his candor when seeking counsel, and I needed it now: What did he think? Could my unwavering belief and trust in others—my optimism—actually pose a risk?

President Tom was again generous with his sage advice. Some strengths, he told me, carried risks that paled in comparison to their potential rewards—and he believed my authentic optimism was one such strength.

"Brad, you're an optimistic person," he said. "It genuinely shows in your voice; you must find a way to hold on to that optimism. If you can, you'll be successful."

His words return to me often, especially on days when I feel discouraged.

Your Authentic Voice

My individual meetings with Protest U staff helped me find my authentic voice and allowed me to begin making strides toward key objectives.

Tony Robbins says a leader's job is to paint an honest picture, never overselling the good or bad.[36] By getting to know my staff, I learned to say what needed to be said honestly and with real compassion.

My authentic voice is rooted in *my* values—of collaboration and care for our shared community. Invariably, these values, consistently applied, foster collegiality and growth.

To do so at Protest U, I took the perspectives of my staff, students, and stakeholders and became their voice with the university's senior administration. But it was a two-way street: I also became senior administration's voice to staff, students, and stakeholders, sharing admin's perspectives and pressures too.

My authentic voice had become one of unwavering optimism and belief in an organization's ability to be successful when working collaboratively, inside and out.

> MY AUTHENTIC VOICE HAD BECOME ONE OF UNWAVERING OPTIMISM AND BELIEF IN AN ORGANIZATION'S ABILITY TO BE SUCCESSFUL WHEN WORKING COLLABORATIVELY, INSIDE AND OUT.

Acknowledging that what I was saying might be hard to hear, I kept my tone positive and assured everyone that we would successfully navigate uncertainty *only* by working together.

I also used my authentic voice to express reason. I rationalized the need for change when necessary, preaching to listeners across the organizational chart. When we could no longer be what we once were, we found our way to new programs and partnerships.

It took time and concerted effort, but the protests ended.

---

36 Robbins, T. (2020). *Business Mastery*. Live event.

Closing Thoughts

Finding your authentic leadership voice requires reflecting on your experiences—and the courage to seek out honest feedback in order to understand your strengths and your gaps. Communicating authentically aids in the process of fearlessly but compassionately saying what needs to be said.

You'll know that you've fully found your authentic voice when what you say aligns with your values, beliefs, and perspectives, nuanced by feedback from constituents on all rungs of the organizational ladder.

As leaders, we must remember that we speak not just for ourselves but also for the organization—indeed, *as* the organization. Therefore, when we speak, people must hear *themselves* in what we say. This plays a huge role in creating—or, done poorly, obstructing—the development of collaborative work cultures, where a pervading sense of shared responsibility drives all stakeholders to address organizational challenges together.

Learning my values and finding my voice were the crucial first steps in my leadership journey. But what did I want the organizations I led to *achieve*? What was my *vision*?

We'll turn to that in chapter 3.

Key Takeaways

This chapter explored reflection as a tool to determining unique leadership strengths and communicating through an authentic voice.

To develop your leadership voice:

• Know and commit to your personal and professional values.

- Listen to colleague feedback about your strengths—and weaknesses.

- Reflect regularly on your interactions to identify areas for improvement.

For Reflection

- Are you living your personal and professional values never, seldom, sometimes, often, or daily?

- Are you receiving feedback? If so, what are you doing to ensure it is honest? If not, how will you develop your "spy" network?

- Some strengths come with potential downsides. What are yours, and which strengths clearly outweigh the risk of applying them?

- Considering these questions, what would your *ideal* authentic voice sound like? Its tone? Its core message? What does it want to promote, achieve, assure, and reinforce?

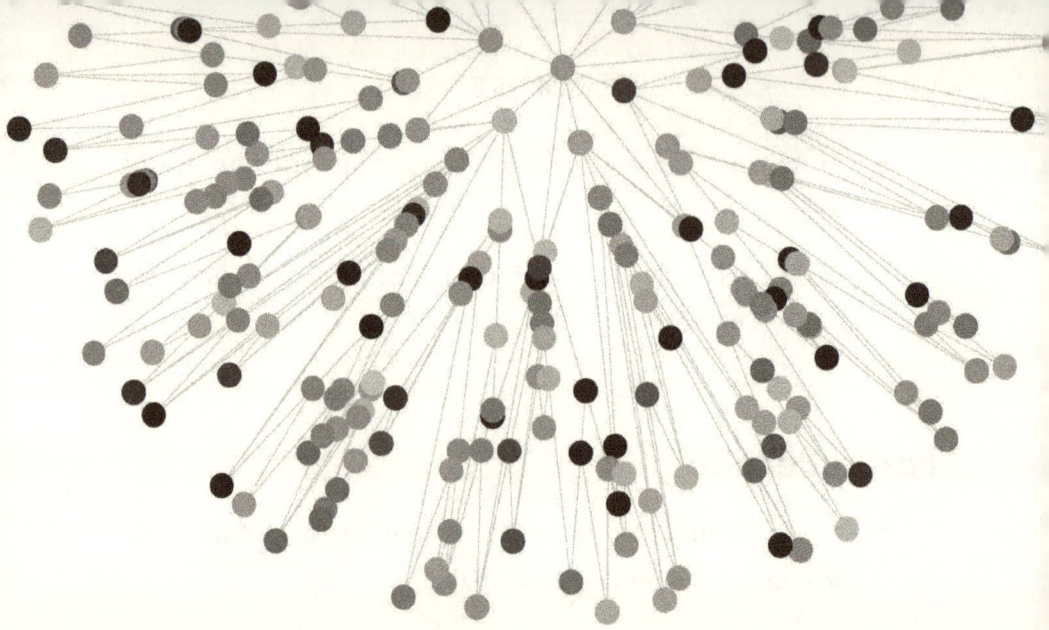

CHAPTER 3

CREATING A VISION

Where there is no vision, the people perish.

—PROVERBS 29:18[37]

Now those kids driving go-karts in chapter 1 were teenagers, with licenses to drive real cars.

Looking back, I enjoyed every minute of this time of life. I had successfully juggled home and work responsibilities, prioritizing family life despite the complexities of shared custody of two children with their mother, and of helping to raise two stepchildren with my second wife.

Our kids' impending "launch into the real world" had professional implications too. It meant I could begin considering the fruits of my professional success and experience: leadership opportunities in other cities.

---

37   Carroll, R., & Prickett, S. (Eds.). (2008). *The Bible: Authorized King James Version*. Oxford Paperbacks.

Offers had been extended throughout the kids' formative years, but I'd rarely considered them, not wanting to disrupt their routines or miss their youths by serving distant institutions.

But now I could toss my hat in the ring, and before long, I sat facing a large interview panel.

What was my vision, they wondered?

I illustrated at length about program excellence, about my track record of fostering elite results, and about how I would transfer those successes to this potential next employer.

It felt a bit odd. Essentially, I recited what the recruiter had outlined for me, the attributes and vision in the job announcement. So it was no surprise when my would-be constituents expressed support and excitement about my vision for restoring the luster of their diminished department.

They offered me the gig: head of performing arts at what I'll call Faraway U.

I wasn't the same person I'd been at the go-kart track. I had grown as a leader: I was confident and excited. After conversations with my wife, ex-wife, and kids, I accepted.

Bring. It. On.

Several months later, I moved and unpacked (somewhat), more than a little eager to begin my next professional chapter.

On my first day, I arrived early, bursting with enthusiasm. I didn't have keys yet, but the music building was open. I entered and slowly wandered around, savoring the moment and feeling exhilarated.

It wouldn't last.

I quickly learned that there was a clear disconnect between the departmental hiring committee's wants and the university's actual direction. Achieving excellence through elite programming requires a substantial financial commitment, one that, it turned out, the university didn't want to make.

That was bad enough, but even basic operations were under-resourced. I seemed to encounter roadblocks everywhere.

But wait! There's more!

Inside the department, morale was low. Enrollments had slowly declined for several years, community partnerships were almost non-existent, and faculty and staff lamented the loss of colleagues who had left seeking greener grass.

Out in the community, I encountered more of the same. As I toured my new city and met with other leaders, I found little engagement with, or even awareness of, the department's activities.

It was like we were invisible.

The hopes of my stakeholders and the vision I had shared during the recruitment process seemed beyond reach. I laid in bed at night, questioning my decision to move—for this. I missed my family and friends. I felt directionless and overwhelmed.

The enthusiasm I had felt for this new adventure—I had even filled my closet with Faraway U swag—vanished.

What had I done?

The Weeds

I was still processing this new reality, yet intuition told me to focus on the department's daily business demands—what some leaders call "the weeds." And I listened, consistently allowing myself to get caught up in immediate issues. I justified that focus by recalling the words of Mike, a mentor from another period of my professional development.

A visionary leader, Mentor Mike generously shared his wisdom at our frequent lunches together. In between bites, I asked him how he "stayed out of the weeds" in realizing his strategic vision. His thoughtful response?

"The thing about weeds is if you don't tend to them, they will kill your garden."

Mic drop.

There was more to his counsel, but I had what I needed for my current situation. My selective memory had validated my recent ground-level efforts.

Focusing on the day-to-day and my open door won me early points with all stakeholders. Everyone appreciated the attention and valued the unlimited access I gave them. I felt like a convenience store—open twenty-four hours a day.

The time in the trenches helped me build rapport, share my values, and lay the foundation for our organizational culture (more on that in part 3). However, it reinforced my sense that something greater was missing.

It was like we were all below deck on a ship, maintaining the engines yet directionless; our only order was "stay afloat." We needed to chart our course. We needed a North Star.

Mentor Mike had also emphasized the need for *balance*—to split time between understanding what's happening on the ground with what's happening at thirty thousand feet. I needed to achieve that balance. I couldn't hide in the weeds any longer.

It reminded me of futurist Alvin Toffler's quote: "You've got to think about big things while you're doing small things."[38] I needed to start thinking big.

---

38   Toffler, A., & Alvin, T. (1980). *The third wave*. Morrow.

Research and Reflection

Discovering where to go requires understanding where you've been. I became curious about, and started learning the history of, my new city, my new organization, and specifically, my new department. There was more than a century of stories.

I leveraged my good rapport with new constituents to create a safe space for honest conversations. I leaned into my strengths; demonstrated nonjudgmental, active listening and empathy; kept my EQ radar on; and used my optimistic voice. I heard varied perspectives about the past and the current state of things. We even mused about the future.

Including stakeholders in these exploratory conversations further strengthened those relationships. Everyone appreciated being a part of the dialogue. I write more about the importance of inclusivity in parts 2 and 3, but for now, it suffices to say that I didn't operate in a silo—my constituents felt heard.

Yet again, I turned to leadership literature for ideas and inspiration.

I've featured the work of Dewar, Keller, and Malhotra prominently thus far, with good reason. In this case, I had taken their suggestion to look back in order to look forward—the idea of creating a vision that draws on a company's heritage.[39]

I turned to stakeholders for history lessons and learned of a time when the music department and concert hall were community hubs, complete with vibrant classrooms and sold-out concerts.

The same authors further advise making the vision about more than money.

The financial challenges were real and known to staff, but I refused to let dollars and cents stifle our imaginations. I allowed myself and

---

39   Dewar, C., Keller, S., & Malhotra, V. (2022).

encouraged others to visualize achievement beyond our means. Our sky was blue.

It was also in this role that I began my early morning reflections. Whatever challenges each day brought, I embraced the morning's solace and went deep into my thoughts.

This time, they returned me to the go-kart track.

In that first leadership role, we found success and produced excellence by prioritizing cooperation and collaboration, which fostered community engagement. We cultivated a network of professionals who valued the development of the next generation of performing artists. We took our music off campus, performing across the city in unusual places, and made the campus an inclusive, welcoming place to all visitors.

I began to see parallels. As my research and reflection deepened, opportunity knocked.

The Haunted Hall

During Faraway U's recruitment process, my final interview included a campus tour led by my future boss. When we arrived at the concert hall, the doors were locked. The space was temporarily closed.

I was disappointed to learn of the hall's woes. It was once a popular venue, but my tour guide explained that the building had been neglected due to the university's financial constraints and shifting strategic priorities. It had not been used for public events for many years; significant renovations would be required to return it to its original shine—not to mention minimum industry standards. A public fundraising campaign was in place but had stalled, with the monetary target far from reach.

He fumbled, finally finding the key, and we entered the historic building.

It was vacant and dark; the power had been cut to allow for electrical work. My research also listed the iconic structure as one of the province's most famous haunted places. Using the modest light from our phones, we clumsily shuffled through the darkness while I tried not to think about the frightening myths.

Soon after I'd started my new role, the electrical work was complete. We resumed modest activity in the building, including reinhabiting a few of its offices. *Cue the opportunity.*

A local concert promoter contacted me. He represented a notable musician, Jeffrey Rempel, and asked about using our concert venue. He was a fan of the historic hall and thought it would be a good fit. Would I consider it?

I remembered the stories about the campus and hall being a vibrant community hub. I loved the idea of seeing the iconic stage shine again, if for just one night. I thought, *Why not?*

People were immediately critical of the idea. I felt frustrated but didn't react. Instead, I turned on my EQ radar and listened. More roadblocks surfaced.

Senior admin felt the event was a distraction from our core business of music education. The money people were critical of donating the hall to our guests. I was even pulled into conversations about security and post-event-cleaning logistics, as our facilities people hadn't had the building on their radar or schedule for some time.

I considered what I'd heard, reflected on my values, and spoke to the concerns.

The promoter, I explained, would provide free tickets to students and staff, helping us build community within our department. I also reasoned that our students should attend professional events to see what was possible and to grow.

Senior admin got on board.

The foot traffic on campus, the venue exposure, and our designation as an event sponsor would benefit our brand, I went on. It was a different *type* of capital, but its value was hard to refute.

The money people got on board.

We were in the middle of a budget year, so I offered to pay for the additional contracted security guards and cleaning staff out of my promotions budget. This helped facilities feel heard, and my contribution helped them hire additional staff.

They climbed aboard too.

We'd worked through people's worries, though my newness likely afforded me a modicum of grace and political capital. I'd wagered everything on the event's success.

The big evening finally came.

Opening Night

It was almost time to head to the hall, located one building over from mine. With my office door open, I noticed two people walking past my doorway and back again. Curious, I stood, walked through my entrance, and entered the hallway just as the couple walked by again.

"May I help?" I asked.

They were lost—they couldn't find the concert hall. "You're so close," I said with a smile. I directed them, and they gratefully rushed on their way.

I strolled farther down the hallway and encountered more lost patrons. I reminded myself that postsecondary campuses are not always the most user-friendly to visitors, but this seemed especially odd. Lost patrons were *everywhere*!

Then it hit me: these patrons were in their twenties and thirties, exactly the demographic of Jeffrey Rempel's fans, and they had *no idea* where the concert hall was! An entire generation, at least, had *never been* there. This historic hall was not a part of their lived history.

The seats filled just in time for the opening number. And though the hall certainly had its shortcomings, its deficiencies seemed endearing to the performers and the sold-out crowd alike.

The next day, the concert was all people talked about.

Students were inspired, faculty and staff were engaged, and the promoter was happy and grateful. Even senior admin, the money people, and the facilities staff were pleased.

Our culture and morale were high. The event had reminded people of what we once were, and the exposure was five-star. We were relevant again.

It was a sign.

By leaning on values of collaboration and cooperation, we found success. We created a win-win external partnership with the promoter that cultivated a positive internal culture and fostered community engagement. We brought people to campus who had never been to the hall. *That* was excellence.

Our North Star was shining. Brightly.

Collaboration and Cooperation

I was a young boy when the original *Battlestar Galactica* television series aired.[40] On the surface, the plot depicted a war in outer space

---

40   Larson, Glen A. (1978). *Battlestar Galactica*. Universal Television.

between humans and robot Cylons, yet I remember being inspired by the show's underlying theme: **community**.

As the last surviving Battlestar, the Galactica assembled and led a motley collection of over two hundred civilian and commercial ships across the galaxy, searching for the mythical planet Earth. The Battlestar protected and supported that "ragtag, fugitive fleet." Little Brad couldn't have known then that the show would become a touchstone of leadership in his adult life.

My department suffered from budget constraints, declining enrollments, decaying and underutilized facilities, departed faculty, and a reputation for being noninclusive. As I toured the city and met with community arts leaders, they, too, spoke of financial struggles and feared the future. It was a familiar saga.

As my career shifted from the concert stage to the classroom and then the boardroom, I became more aware of the struggles that the performing arts and arts education programs experience. It was common to hear about grant funding cuts to community arts organizations, orchestras in financial crisis, and underfunded or closed postsecondary programs.

Everyone was competing for the same diminishing resources. I remembered more of Mentor Mike's words: "When the watering hole starts to shrink, the animals start to look at each other differently." Sadly, this summed up the challenges the arts were facing.

Yet it felt like a time when we needed to cooperate rather than compete. My department might be the catalyst for such collaboration—a Battlestar, if you will.

I had a vision.

Envisioning Your Vision

I have practiced visualization for many years now. Remember Sharon, my guitar professor? She introduced me to this tool, as we addressed my stage fright.

I would begin by visualizing everything about an impending performance: waiting backstage, the sight of the house lights being brought up to full, my pace as I confidently walked onto the stage, my short bow acknowledging the applause, the entire performance, the full bow recognizing the audience's approval, and my turn and exit off the stage into the darkness of the wings. Visualization became part of my success formula, and I was about to use it again, this time to clarify my vision for our department.

During my reflective early mornings, sometimes I left my office and slowly strolled the quiet buildings. I visualized vibrant, buzzing hallways, full classrooms, and a sold-out concert hall. I remembered George Lucas's words: "You can't do it unless you imagine it."[41] And I visualized my goal: making our department relevant again.

I imagined our school as a beacon for all—a nucleus for the performing arts, where everyone was welcome. One day, I thought, it would be difficult to meet a person in the city who hadn't had some interaction with our department.

And I immediately started communicating that vision.

---

41 Attributed to George Lucas.

Energize and Inspire: Paint a Picture of the Future

Armed with a clear vision rooted in my values, I used my authentic voice to advocate for, onboard stakeholders to, and paint an optimistic picture of the future.

In a recent paper, Nufer Yasin Ates et al. explain that visionary leadership can successfully enact strategic change by showing *why* the change is needed, which often persuades and inspires people to embrace the change.[42] Still, there were challenges.

A new vision typically requires some level of change, which can create anxiety among constituents. I leaned on my strengths, trusted my intuition, and listened, ensuring those with concerns were heard.

I also engaged change management theory, through the iconic John Kotter, absorbing his life's research on leading organizational change. Kotter's seminal work on organizational change management—his eight-step process—filled in my gaps.[43] My vision in hand, I drew on Kotter's advice that stakeholders must be *empowered to act* on the vision once it has been created and communicated.[44]

And communicate it, I did.

Mentor Mike once told me, "Every speaking engagement is an opportunity to share your vision." So every chance I got, I used my authentic voice to share my vision, always connecting it to my values. This gave my team and stakeholders clarity, energized them, and

---

42   Ates, N. Y., Tarakci, M., Porck, J., Knippenberg, D., & Groenen, P. (2019). Why visionary leadership fails. *Harvard Business Review*.

43   Kotter, J. P. (1996). Why transformation efforts fail. *Harvard Business Review*.

44   Kotter, J. P., Kim, W. C., & Mauborgne, R. A. (2011). *HBR's 10 must reads on change management (including featured article "Leading Change," by John P. Kotter)*. Harvard Business Press.

provided direction. Over time, my vision became *our* vision, and our vision became our identity.

I remembered another mentor's advice: "Write like the king; talk like the people." So I strived to always use the appropriate tone.

For example, my tone was more formal in emails, conversational when speaking with staff and students in the hallways, assured when giving remarks at an event, personal and engaging with a donor over lunch, and welcoming when anyone walked through my office's open door.

It's harder to label the voice I used when conversing at the urinals (seriously), but the fact that I was approached even there shows how encompassing our vision had become.

And then it became a reality.

We fostered excellence by partnering with the city's philharmonic orchestra, providing them a place to rehearse in exchange for complimentary concert tickets for students. We also opened it to guest classes led by the orchestra's principal players.

We brought diversity to our concert hall by befriending the city's folk festival and other professional presenters.

OVER TIME, MY VISION BECAME *OUR* VISION, AND OUR VISION BECAME OUR IDENTITY.

We worked with area school boards to bring high school music students to campus and sent our faculty into the community's schools.

We even partnered with the city's professional football team; our students provided halftime entertainment at all home games.

We supported amateur performing arts organizations by opening our space for rehearsals. When the bewildered yet grateful organizations asked what we wanted in exchange, I asked them to share our logo on their website and identify us as a supporter, sponsor, and friend.

And I asked that they share our vision so it might spread far and wide: *The performing arts are for everyone—elite to amateur, competitive to recreational.*

The campus buzzed like an awakened beehive. We injected a palpable vibrance into our spaces, thanks to our dozens of diverse partnerships. The "traffic" on campus was exciting, especially around our historic concert hall, which brought tens of thousands of visitors to campus.

The old icon was relevant again.

Our vision was about more than money, but the busy spaces improved those metrics, too, generating increased enrollment and a stronger bottom line.

As I walked the hallways and poked my head into classrooms and rehearsal spaces, the enthusiasm was tangible. I thought of the legendary punk rocker Johnny Ramone, who always wanted his guitar to sound like energy coming out of the amplifier—not even like music—just energy.[45] *That's* what our *campus* sounded like!

My early morning reflections had manifested: we had become the Battlestar for performing arts in our city!

Stop the Presses

Teenage Brad watched MuchMusic. A lot.

Like the United States' MTV (Music Television), MuchMusic was Canada's twenty-four-hour music video channel. As a wannabe rock star, I especially enjoyed the interviews with my heroes, including hearing their stories—how they'd "made it."

---

45   Coelho, V. (Ed.). (2003). *The Cambridge companion to the guitar*. Cambridge University Press.

CHAPTER 3

I remember a Q&A with Poison's Bret Michaels. Although the band had sold millions of albums, the interviewer was more interested in the band's press related to nonmusic topics: their outrageous image and offstage antics.

Undaunted, Michaels replied, "As long as they print your name right and put your picture in there, I don't think you can go wrong."[46] Perhaps his words were tongue in cheek, but they always resonated with me and echoed P. T. Barnum's famous quote: "There's no such thing as bad publicity."[47]

More than once, my boss at Faraway U, with a wary smile, had told me, "I don't ever want to see you on the front page of the newspaper." Translation: He embraced neither Michaels's nor Barnum's theorems. He never wanted to see a scandalous headline or other bad press for the university.

Well, we made the front page.

Our Battlestar had become a civic leader in community engagement. The newspaper article (and photo) discussed the historic concert hall's resurgence as a communal arts hub. The department was praised for its inclusive collaboration. The story used the voices and experiences of community beneficiaries to amplify the message and impact.

The article also drew attention to the neglected venue. Six months after our front-page splash, an eight-figure private and public joint-funding initiative was announced. The historic concert hall would be restored to serve future generations. And the ghost stories would continue.

Michaels, B. (1988). "Poison's Bret Michaels and Rikki Rockett talk to Steve Anthony on MuchMusic." MuchMusic, retrieved from https://www.youtube.com/watch?v=Bzhe322yW7w

47 Kunhardt, P. B., & Kunhardt, P. W. (1995). *P.T. Barnum: America's greatest showman.* Knopf.

Living on 10

We'd achieved success of our vision, but the road was not easy. There were difficult days.

Those early morning reflection sessions could be challenging—determining my values, finding my voice, seeking my vision. It took sustained daily focus and dedication.

Still, despite my best intentions and preparation, things could go sideways fast. As the former heavyweight boxing champion Mike Tyson said, "Everyone has a plan until they get punched in the face."[48]

I may not have been physically beaten, but I experienced circumstances that challenged my optimism and, at least temporarily, curbed my enthusiasm. Some days, the outside noise overwhelmed my values, voice, and vision. In those times I reflected, returned inward, and asked myself: What could I control? The answer was always the same: me—my attitude, my effort, and my actions.

Here in part 1, I have shared my reflection process: making the time, which is essential for contemplation, because the journey toward success in leadership starts inside oneself. As mine has continued, I've added another reflection period at day's end, evaluating the one thing I fully control: myself.

Had I lived my values that day? Been present in each interaction? What attitude had I brought to the day? I even evaluated myself on a scale of 1 to 10.

It proved to be a game changer.

I challenged myself to bring the same energy and enthusiasm to each day. I recognized that I always had a choice. Earning a 10 of 10 for my attitude, effort, and actions was possible *every* day—it was up to me, and it became more than my goal. It was what I expected of myself.

---

48   Tyson, M. (2013). *Undisputed truth*. Penguin.

But how *exactly*—and to what ends—have I applied this principle? Where and how did I help build great outcomes for the programs, colleagues, and institutions I've worked with?

Here's a hint: **community**. *Stick around to learn more in part 2.*

Closing Thoughts

As leaders, our job is to see the path that others do not see.

Strategic vision requires research, and time for reflection. Without them, it is difficult at best to visualize the future—to find your North Star. Connecting your vision to your values through your voice lays the foundation for values-based leadership and ensures that we inhabit the high ground.

> AS LEADERS, OUR JOB IS TO SEE THE PATH THAT OTHERS DO NOT SEE.

Sharing a leadership vision can be inspiring for all—the leader and stakeholders. Lean into your leadership strengths and use your voice to communicate a strategic vision aligned with your values. Use that vision to energize your team and provide them with a road map. Soon, your vision will become theirs as well, fostering engagement inside the organization and out in the community.

Key Takeaways

This chapter explored the importance of envisioning goals and creating a clear vision to provide a road map for the team.

- Your strategic vision emerges through research and reflection.

- Your vision provides direction and alignment.

- Communicating your vision inspires collaboration among all stakeholders.

For Reflection

Envisioning your goals creates a clear vision of the future. Set aside thirty minutes this week for self-reflection. Imagine your desired future and write a one- or two-sentence vision statement. Review it against your values and evaluate its alignment with your vision.

At each day's end, reflect on your engagement. Here's the scale I use:

- 10 = I left it all on the stage with no regrets.

- 8–9 = It was a strong day, with only a few minor slips.

- 6–7 = There were a few highlights, but I lacked consistency.

- 5 and lower = Today was a struggle; I'll be better tomorrow.

Notice which reflections are associated with higher and lower scores. What is your daily goal? Is it 8 out of 10? Is it 10 out of 10? Why? Remember, for some sports teams, anything short of a championship means a failed season. For others, just making the playoffs is a huge accomplishment. Where will you set *your* bar?

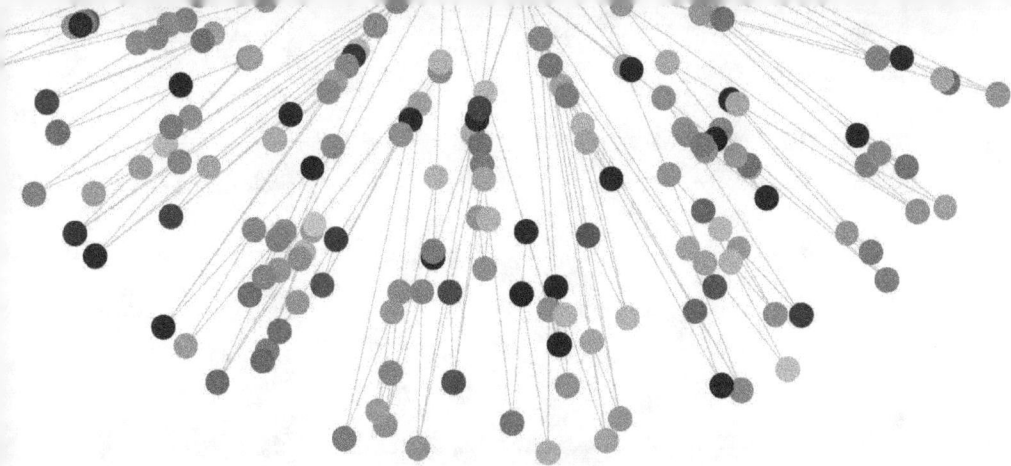

PART 2

FOSTERING COMMUNITY CONNECTIONS

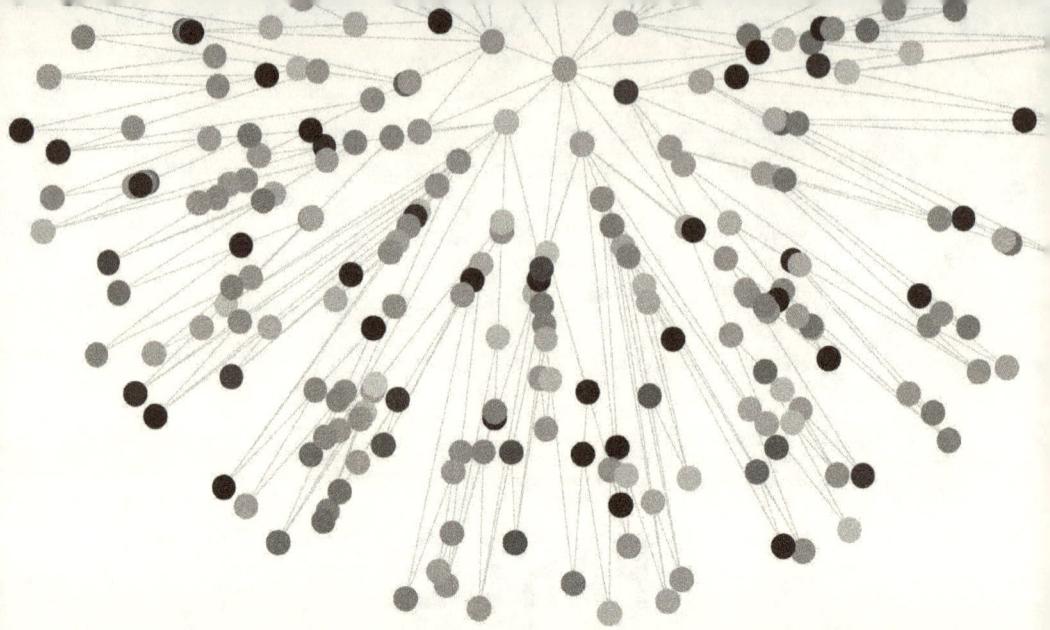

CHAPTER 4

BE VISIBLE, MAKE CONNECTIONS

Eighty percent of success is showing up.

—WOODY ALLEN[49]

In my first six months as president and CEO of Grasslands College, I invested considerable time touring all six of its campuses. I got to know the faculty and staff, met with students, and was generally visible. This provided opportunities to connect.

I also made it a point to meet external stakeholders in each of our communities save one: the town of Hazlet. And I justified my absence—to myself, at least.

Soon after I started my new gig, a rumor reached me: the college was planning to close the Hazlet campus. Indeed, it seemed folks were waiting for the new leader—me—to make the final decision and close the book.

---

49 Safire, W. (1989). On language; the Elision Fields. *New York Times*, 13.

I felt both surprised and unnerved.

"Really?" I thought. "My first major move as president is going to be academia's equivalent of corporate downsizing?" There had been no mention of this before my arrival. Was it somewhere in my contract's fine print?

I took a breath and became curious. I'd soon learn that the college had been withdrawing from Hazlet for years—closing programs, retiring and relocating staff, and reducing its community engagement. Even the annual par-three golf tournament, Grasslands's sponsorship of which signaled its commitment to the community, had been abandoned. The news, my spies confirmed, was all over Hazlet: residents suspected, even *expected*, the campus's closure.

Further confirmation came when the town's representative on our board of governors approached me after the gavel had fallen on our first meeting.

"Sorry, Brad," he said. "I'm stepping down." He could read the surprise and concern on my face; I valued his contributions, and we enjoyed a good rapport. "I can't be a part of this," he continued. "I can't be on the board when we close the Hazlet campus. I still need to live and work in the community."

I understood his dilemma. I was saddened but respected his choice. Yet it wasn't just Hazlet residents who were talking; staff were consumed by the imminent closure too.

Remember Vince, my vice president? He advocated for closing Hazlet with a cool disregard. His callousness left me uneasy, but I get it—sometimes hard business decisions must be made. This one would impact an entire community, though. "He can't even fake compassion," I thought. It was just cold.

In the face of what was clearly an open secret, I was reluctant to connect with the Hazlet community. Yet as it so reliably does, reflecting on the situation offered insight. I recognized I wasn't being true to my values.

"Close the campus?" I thought. "Brad, you haven't even tried to save it!"

In this case, reflection took me back to my first marriage. The relationship was struggling. We went to counseling, tried more date nights, and even adventured to a tropical destination to save the union. Ultimately, the marriage failed, and I'm the last to suggest that any type of divorce is easy. Yet knowing we had *tried* allowed us to go our separate ways without regret.

I needed to take the same approach now.

Hazlet, pack your suitcase and remember your bathing suit; we're going on a hot holiday!

Six months into my new job, I told the executive staff that I'd be visiting Hazlet later that week. I had invited the town's mayor to join me on campus to visit with students, faculty, and staff, I explained, and Mayor Miller had accepted and returned my invitation, to be his guest at the town council meeting that same night.

"He told me they haven't heard from the college in some time," I added.

My announcement was met with an awkward silence. Finally, someone spoke up: "It's gonna be rough—they're gonna be tough on you." Though I maintained my resolve outwardly, on the inside, my confidence wavered. I imagined negative outcomes and wondered, "Is my health insurance current?"

Visibility Is Essential for Engagement

In junior high school, I won the attendance award each year.

It's not the kind of award that's displayed in the school's trophy case or to which monuments are erected on the front lawn. I'm pretty sure that even my parents skipped the annual awards ceremonies. Still, it taught Little Brad an early lesson: showing up is a key ingredient in success.

Being visible in school allowed me to connect and create meaningful relationships with my teachers and peers. It's a habit I've maintained throughout my career—from the go-kart track to the haunted hall—and in my experience, **visibility** is the essential first step toward engagement.

Our college lacked visibility in Hazlet. And as my first days and weeks became months, I'd learn that Hazlet was a microcosm of what was happening at many of the college's campus communities.

One of my favorite cinematic moments comes in 1992's *A Few Good Men*, starring Tom Cruise and Jack Nicholson.[50] In the courtroom drama's climactic scene, Cruise's character, a prosecutor, baits Nicholson's into admitting his guilt. The spectacular moment—culminating in Nicholson's terse admonition to Cruise's character, "You can't handle the truth!"—is what hooked me on legal dramas.

As I investigated Grasslands College's reduced community engagement in Hazlet, I channeled my inner prosecutor.

Exhibit A: Having lunch with the mayor in another of our campus communities, I requested his candor. "How's our visibility?" I asked. He didn't hold back: "You have no presence in our community. None." Obviously, lunch was on me—like the egg on my face.

Exhibit B: Upon meeting the new campus manager at another of our communities, he confessed, "I've spent my entire career in education, and I'd never heard of the college until I saw the job ad

---

50   Reiner, R. (1992). *A few good men*. Columbia Pictures.

for this position." My staff balked at his remarks, but his testimony rang true to my ears.

Exhibit C: At another of our campus communities, staff admitted that when local residents refer to "the college," they're usually referencing the larger one thirty minutes west in the next city. The story was anecdotal but again rang true. Evidence admitted.

Exhibit D: At a conference organized by a professional organization, an attendee—a seasoned business leader—read my name tag. Puzzled, she asked, "Where are your campuses located?" I explained that we had locations in two of the bedroom communities just outside the city where we both stood. She'd never heard of us.

But here's my favorite.

Exhibit E: At a town forum, the facilitator asked the assembled community and business leaders, "What is our town's value proposition to current and prospective residents? Why live or move here?" Attendees began calling out answers: "We have a hospital." "Indoor swimming pool." On and on they went.

Soon, the facilitator had a sizable list on her flip chart. Finally, someone said, "The college. We have a college in our town."

It took *twelve minutes*, and somebody had even mentioned *the dog park* before our campus!

The gavel dropped. Bang! Guilty.

The college's low visibility in the communities it served could be neatly summed up in one of my mom's favorite truisms: "Out of sight, out of mind."[51]

So how, the question became, did we get Grasslands *front* of mind?

---

51 Brad's mom.

Be a Water Buffalo

I must admit that for decades, I had a negative perception of service clubs. I blame *The Flintstones*.

Arriving home after school as a child, I immediately turned on the television. Without fail, that staple in children's programming appeared, and I closely followed the antics of Fred Flintstone, Barney Rubble, and the rest of the gang.[52] Most curious to me was the two lead characters' membership in the Loyal Order of Water Buffaloes—a fraternal, male-only organization that always seemed to be up to more nonsense than good sense.

Yet upon surveying Grassland's disengaged communities, I had no option but to acknowledge the dire situation and swallow my preconceptions.

I joined a service club.

The club's Friday lunches proved to be a reliable, low-key way to meet business owners and community leaders. The atmosphere was pleasant and the conversations friendly, and our networking linked me to other events, activities, and organizations—more opportunities to increase our visibility. While, I'll hasten to add, meeting some of the nicest people I've ever had the privilege to know.

The college already belonged to the chambers of commerce in each of our campus communities, and I attended those meetings and events as well, embracing any chance to show up and engage. I soon had a full dance card each week and quickly became Mr. Visibility.

When I wasn't actively participating in engagement, I was studying engagement literature, just as I'd turned to leadership texts early in my management career.

---

52   Barbera, J., & Hanna, W. *The Flintstones*. American Broadcasting Company.

Winston Tinglin and Donna Joyette, authors with a lifetime of public- and private-sector community engagement experience, see being visible as the preparation stage for creating a positive first contact.[53] Just by showing up, I created the opportunity for those initial conversations.

Douglas Reeves, Nancy Frey, and Douglas Fisher, authors of *Confronting the Crisis of Engagement*, write that event attendance demonstrates making an investment in your community.[54] As I would learn, the return on my time investment was the cultivation of trust, which in turn laid the foundation for more deliberate, professional conversations.

Makara Rumley, author of *Modern-Day Strategies for Community Engagement*, believes trust must be established for a deeper conversation about collaboration to occur.[55] Overall, I had cultivated an environment for those deeper discussions, where I used my voice to share my values and vision.

Now it was time to go deeper.

From Visibility to Participation

I don't like golf. There, I said it. I know the rules of the game, and I own clubs (my late father's set, which he bought secondhand—the woods are actually *made of wood*).

53   Tinglin, W., & Joyette, D. (2020). *Community engagement in a changing social landscape*. FriesenPress.

54   Reeves, D., Frey, N., & Fisher, D. (2022). *Confronting the crisis of engagement: Creating focus and resilience for students, staff, and communities*. Corwin Press.

55   Rumley, M. (2020). *Modern-day strategies for community engagement*. Purposely Created.

My golf swing resembles a slap shot (Adam Sandler pretty much captured it in *Happy Gilmore*).[56] Yet during my second summer as president of Grasslands, I participated in every community golf tournament in the region. Why? I wanted to amplify my presence through deeper, more deliberate participation in community events, which increased my visibility.

That same summer, we also had floats in every municipal parade. *OK, "float" is a stretch*—we had a bright-red truck with the college's name on the doors. When I wasn't driving the truck and waving out the window, I ran alongside it, handing candy to the crowd.

Meanwhile, at my service club, I was being asked to speak on one topic or another on a regular basis. Simply because I *showed up* on a regular basis. My participation led to greater visibility for the college.

Author and keynote speaker Amanda Lea Kaiser writes that participation is one of the natural and necessary early stages of successful community engagement.[57] As leaders, we must never be above rolling up our sleeves and doing what's needed. Doing so makes us visible and leads to genuine, lasting community connection.

> WHY? I WANTED TO AMPLIFY MY PRESENCE THROUGH DEEPER, MORE DELIBERATE PARTICIPATION IN COMMUNITY EVENTS, WHICH INCREASED MY VISIBILITY.

Through such participation and connection, Grasslands took the next step: helping to lead the communities we serve.

---

56   Dugan, D. (1996). *Happy Gilmore*. Universal Pictures.

57   Kaiser, A. L. (2023). *Elevating engagement: Uncommon strategies for creating a thriving member community*. PageTwo.

From Participation to Sponsorship

We've seen that *being* seen is the first step toward engagement, and that it unlocks the door to participation. Sponsorship is the natural outgrowth of both and, done right, is what builds and maintains an organization's visibility in the community it serves.

> AND IT ALL STARTED WITH SIMPLY *SHOWING UP.*

At Grasslands, we soon began sponsoring the chamber of commerce's business excellence awards, recognizing the contributions of other organizations to our community. This allowed me to say a few words about the college before announcing one of the award winners.

Having already embarrassed myself on their links, it was a short jump to sponsoring an annual golf tournament in each of our communities, and a host of other events throughout the years. Sponsorships like these provided our brand greater visibility—and not just through the promotional materials we'd distribute liberally at such events. Increasingly, they became a platform for sharing our values and mission.

Before long, I could walk into any room, it seemed, and immediately engage in conversations that lasted for hours. I was no longer the new president of Grasslands, but simply "Brad from the college." I knew my outreach was working when a friend sent a text message with a photo of me speaking at an event we sponsored. "You're everywhere!" he playfully teased.

"No," I thought. " *The college* is everywhere."

And it all started with simply *showing up.*

Quantity Leads to Quality

You can do anything, but you can't do everything. You don't know what you don't know.

Those platitudes guided my first year as president at Grasslands, following a format I had used in previous posts. I'd figured out that the first year is less strategic; it's about volume and visibility. I'd attend any event, play golf, walk in a parade, volunteer to be in a dunk tank, anything—once at least. I needed to experience each occasion for myself and decide if it was worth the investment. I didn't let others influence my attendance, one way or the other.

Remember the community forum, Lawyer Brad's *Exhibit E,* where it took twelve minutes for the college to be called out as an asset to the community? Staff told me the event was "below my pay grade" and I shouldn't waste my time on it. Yet sitting in that forum for those twelve minutes waiting for someone to finally say "the college" was a crucial moment. It affirmed my intuition and set alight my desire to alter our community narrative.

After each event, I spent my early mornings, as you might expect, reflecting on and ultimately concluding which events offered the best return on my investment.

Other Perspectives

Given my lifelong passion for community engagement, I regularly mention it when "talking shop" with other leaders, across sectors. As a dean, I talked to my counterpart at another university, a woman much more seasoned than I. She said, "It really matters when you show up at events. People notice."

She was right.

Over my long career, I have observed various leaders apply various styles of community visibility. As a college guitar instructor, I remember our director appearing at events. It created a buzz. "He's here!" It *mattered*. It made our event feel important.

Remember the angry parents who waited for me in the parking lot? When I attended the dance shows and competitions, the parents were kind to me; they put aside their differences and welcomed me. They appreciated me showing up.

In that same role, as I was managing that performing arts department, the college's senior leadership never came to our events—or any school events, for that matter. Sure, they were in the office Monday to Friday during the day, and some had open doors. But you wouldn't see them at campus events or proudly representing the college out in the community, especially after hours. We all noticed, and it hurt our brand.

Big Day in Hazlet

On the day of our meeting at the Hazlet campus, Mayor Miller was gracious and thoughtful as he interacted with the students and staff. We then talked in the boardroom—for two hours.

I confessed my feelings of uncertainty since learning about the potential closing of the campus. He could tell it was weighing on me, and his graciousness again came to the fore.

"Brad," Mayor Miller concluded, "it's *all* of our responsibility to make this campus thrive."

As planned, I attended Hazlet's town council that night and was welcomed with warmth and enthusiasm. Our conversation was solution-focused, and throughout, the councilors were supportive and encouraging.

So, too, was just about everyone in the restaurant where the mayor and I had dinner after the council meeting, and still more discussion. The reception I received when Mayor Miller introduced me to other diners and the staff—he knew them all—was humbling and mirrored the mayor's own graciousness.

Wanting to experience more of the town's culture, I postponed the two-hour drive home and stayed in the local motel that night. The next day, I had breakfast at another local restaurant.

I left Hazlet feeling inspired.

One month later, I organized a scholarship reception where local donors met the students whom their contributions were supporting. We held the event on campus to bring the community through our doors and contracted a local restaurant for catering. Mayor Miller provided opening remarks, after which I expressed my gratitude for their investment in our mission and engaged each of them personally.

The event was a success. Next, I contacted the group that had taken over the par-three golf tournament.

All sponsorship opportunities were filled for the year, so I took the only option remaining: I agreed to be a hole-in-one "scrutineer." I sat by the green, literally dodging golf balls while ensuring the integrity of the pricey five-figure hole-in-one cash prize. As foursomes left the green after holing out, I approached from the trees (not as creepy as it sounds), introduced myself, and handed out some college swag, interacting with every golfer—and managing to avoid injury from errant drives.

The visibility was exceptional.

Later that summer, I spent a day popping in on our Hazlet donors at their places of business.

Always mindful of the sanctity of their workplaces, I entered each business with a bag of swag, introduced myself to whoever happened to greet me, and thanked them for supporting our college. The owner or leader often came forward for a quick handshake and brief conversation.

I even dropped muffins and doughnuts at the town administration offices. Again, I kept my EQ radar on, aware that I was showing up unannounced on their turf—so I kept these visibility visits brief.

Every now and then came a breakthrough, and there's a particular one I'll always remember.

Entering this donor's business, I scanned the room for a familiar face and heard, "Hey, Brad." I looked over. Her face was familiar—I had met so many people in Hazlet—but *what was her name?*

She smiled, recognizing my uncertainty. "I'm Amanda; we met at the scholarship event and the golf course." My mind raced. *Yes.* Now I remembered. But wait, she knew *me*! People in Hazlet *knew* me! And if they knew me, *they knew the college*!

I kept my foot on the gas, participating in Hazlet's Fall Festival, Winter Light-Up, and Santa Claus Parade. I connected with the local high school principal. I learned first names—from restaurant owners to gas station attendants. I started to receive invitations from local leaders to their niche community events.

Finally, our English Language Program presented a semester-ending event—a spelling bee. It was a fun way to showcase the students' hard work over the term. I attended without expectations, other than supporting the students, faculty, and staff.

What happened next was affirming.

I arrived to a full parking lot and found myself wondering what else was happening. Inside, the hallways were buzzing, and finding a seat in the venue was difficult. When the bee began, it was standing room only. The local media were on hand, as were Mayor Miller and the local elected members of the provincial government.

The event filled my heart. The crowd roared as each student spelled their words. At a reception afterward, I sat at the back of the room, enjoying a small plate of goodies, watching the interactions, and feeling the energy. I recalled Mayor Miller's words at our first meeting: the campus's success is down to all of us.

Together, we'd done it—built a community of shared ownership.

My schedule was demanding, so in between face-to-face interactions in Hazlet, I stayed "visible" with emails, thank-you cards, engagement on social media, phone conversations, and voice messages. All can keep the fire warm, but no flame burns more brightly than in-person engagement.

One year later, we doubled our program offerings and tripled enrollment in Hazlet. The year after that, we were running short of classroom space. Talk of closing the campus had become a distant dot in our rearview mirror.

Closing Thoughts

Visibility is essential for engagement.

Participation in local organizations and attendance at community events is just the start. Once people see you, they want to know who you are, what you do, and why you're there.

By answering these questions and learning others' answers to them, you represent your organization and increase its community connections. Quantity is important early on, to expand your network and to learn where interests overlap. Over time, you can narrow your direct points of focus but remain widely visible, thus maximizing the relationships that benefit all involved while preserving a broader community presence.

Valuing community engagement has contributed to my professional success. My lived experiences are not unique; as Harvard Business School's Jeffrey Bussgang and author Jono Bacon write, community engagement helps move the needle on corporate success.[58]

Forbes writer Michael Timmes believes community involvement keys business success, by helping to raise an organization's public profile and contributing to building corporate culture (more in part 3).[59]

VISIBILITY IS A VITAL INVESTMENT.

In my new role at Grasslands, after one year of active engagement, all six of our campus communities increased enrollment, with one achieving its highest enrollment in seven years.

While driving to the many events I participated in, my mind often flashed through my many to-dos, deadlines, and deliverables. I could easily come up with an excuse to stop the car, turn around, and send regrets. Instead, I adopted the Nike slogan: "Just Do It."[60]

When you're a leader, stakeholders and constituents understand your time's demands. This makes your appearance *even more valuable*. Being visible in a busy, noisy world is appreciated; making connections matters. Show up, engage, and connect—visibility is a vital investment.

The Woody Allen quote atop this chapter is well known, but I prefer Hillary Clinton's variation: "Showing up is not all of life, but it counts for a lot."[61] As we've seen, showing up has been a powerful tool for me. Being visible was the critical first step in engaging our communities.

---

58   Bussgang, J., & Bacon, J. (2020). When community becomes your competitive advantage. *Harvard Business Review*.

59   Timmes, M. (2023). Why community involvement supports business success. *Forbes*. Retrieved from https://www.forbes.com/sites/forbescoachescouncil/2023/07/11/why-community-involvement-supports-business-success/?sh=7dc4666a22fc

60   Nike. (1988). Retrieved from https://www.nike.com/ca/

61   Clinton, H. (2009). *Putting the elements of smart power into practice.* Retrieved from https://2009-2017.state.gov/secretary/20092013clinton/rm/2009a/02/119411.htm

The next step is understanding what your community *wants*. We'll take that step in chapter 5.

Key Takeaways

In this chapter, we've discussed the power of showing up and being visible. This is critical for making connections.

- Community engagement begins with showing up—and introducing yourself often.

- Next comes participation. Get out there consistently to expand your connections.

- Sponsorship of community events raises organizational visibility and enhances stature.

- Quantity first, then quality. But even as you reduce contact quantity, stay connected in other ways (like emails and phone calls).

For Reflection

List ten local organizations or events to engage with over the next three months. Schedule these events and meetings, and after attending, reflect on the contacts made and relationships built. Identify the next steps for strengthening these relationships.

Employ a process that tracks your interactions, including contact information and personal and professional details. Build an events calendar, remembering that the most impactful events typically recur annually. Develop a system for tracking the effectiveness of your attendance at given events and to identify future opportunities to increase your organization's visibility and community engagement.

CHAPTER 5

WHAT DOES YOUR COMMUNITY VALUE?

There is no power for change greater than a community discovering what it cares about.

—MARGARET J. WHEATLEY[62]

"No more status quo," I was told.

I'd heard it several times. The board wanted me to bring fresh ideas in order to innovate. I felt confident I could deliver on this directive as the new president of Grasslands College.

I had experience in innovation. As dean at Protest U, my team and I successfully diversified our historic offerings by pioneering novel programs and forging new internship agreements with global companies. These steps helped us fulfill our dual objectives: serving students and meeting labor market demand.

---

62 Wheatley, M. J. (2002). "Willing to be disturbed." In *Turning to one another: Simple conversations to restore hope to the future.* Berrett-Koshler Publishers, Inc.

They also attracted national media attention, as partnerships with industry and other schools were considered innovative in themselves. That attention elevated our school's brand and made me something of a campus celebrity.

Departing that role, I found that my conversations with these partners included musing about continuing our symbiotic relationships at my new institution. I was sure we would, as many of these people had also become my friends. I felt ready to revolutionize my new college and its community.

Go, innovation!

My first months as president were a blur of histories studied, stories heard, and data consumed. Topics fueling my early morning reflection included declining domestic enrollments, decreased government funding, demand for more classroom resources, diminished community engagement, a recent employee survey that found low staff morale, and the harsh realities of the rising costs of doing business.

It wasn't pretty.

It triggered in me a sense of urgency. I wanted to fix everything … *by the following Tuesday.* I forgot about the blueprint for success that I had been developing over my career and instead began reconnecting with my former partners at Protest U.

I thought of James Cameron's theatrical hits *Terminator 2: Judgement Day*[63] and *Aliens,*[64] in which stars Arnold Schwarzenegger and Sigourney Weaver again headlined their respective blockbuster sequels, which far exceeded both franchises' strong debuts. Maybe we could collaborate at my new institution and create blockbuster sequels too.

Lights, camera, action!

---

63   Cameron, J. (1991). *Terminator 2: Judgment day.* Tri-Star Pictures.

64   Cameron, J. (1986). *Aliens.* 20th Century Fox.

Yet as I conversed with my former associates, questions about my new community compounded, leading to a stark realization: I didn't yet know what this community valued.

The partnerships back at Protest U were successful because together, we responded to specific community needs aligned with the community's values, which in turn aligned with our values. Here at Grasslands, though, gaps in my understanding led me to make incorrect assumptions about this new community's priorities and values.

Perhaps I should say "*these* new communities," as Grasslands maintains several campuses across its provincial home.

It was a sobering moment, realizing that until I knew what most mattered to these communities, I could not effectively engage them.

Finding Friends

The television series *Friends* was a pop culture phenomenon, producing ten seasons that aired from 1994 to 2004.[65] The situation comedy was wildly successful during its original run on NBC, constantly in the top ten for viewership and recognized with numerous industry awards. It would eclipse that impressive success in syndication and, decades later, is still a staple on streaming platforms.

So what was such a famed show about? What was its plot?

As its title suggests, the show was about *friendship*. It followed six friends navigating life's journey together, supporting each other through their highs and lows. Fundamentally, it showed the impact of friendship and drew upon the value our society places on loyalty and connection.

That's what this new role of mine needed: friends.

---

65 Crane, D., & Kauffman, M. (1994–2004). *Friends*. NBC.

The differences between a single-campus university in a large urban center to a college with six rural campuses were obvious and presented quite the learning curve. As Grasslands's president, I spent much of my first year traveling, being visible, and especially, *listening*.

On each campus, I heard of ongoing struggles with sustainability, including recruitment and retaining of students and employees.

Off campus, I leveraged my visibility to build trust, enabling, over time, candid conversations with elected officials and community and business leaders—in every community we served.

I still had much to learn, but one of my early insights was to resist painting the six places with the same brush. Though they share a provincial home, community priorities differ in each municipality, as do our student bodies and staff cultures.

Researching these communities became my passion. I studied local history, from economic cycles and weather trends to sports successes and political tenures. I researched community organizations, events, municipal celebrations and festivities, chamber of commerce and other business-sector happenings, and local sports teams' schedules. I watched for political functions, fairs, festivals, and fundraisers.

Social media was an effective tool. I followed various organizations' and individuals' social media accounts and "liked" posts and events they promoted, engaging with them and encouraging their engagement with Grasslands. But as detailed in chapter 4, I knew that I had to be more than just *virtually* visible.

I worked each community network in person, making one-to-one connections that led to deeper conversations. Experience had taught me that by working to understand what each of our communities valued, I'd also learn who might partner with the college in each of those communities.

So I began to look for friends.

I started with people and organizations that already had relations with the college, including elected officials, donors, and sponsors. I quickly learned that the overall health of many of these relationships varied.

Being the new president, I could convey my limited understanding of a current or past connection between our organizations and express gratitude for that relationship. I could declare my genuine desire to stay supportive of each other as we moved ahead.

Such petitions were always met with outward positivity, yet it was clear in some cases that scar tissue from past organizational interactions remained.

One of these cases was a lunch meeting with the mayor of one of our campus communities. We met at our downtown campus and walked the town's busy main street. We'd met the prior month when he popped over to campus for a coffee, and the month before, when I visited his town council. Our rapport had grown quickly.

Now, settled in his restaurant of choice over lunch, the conversation was coming easily—until he surprised me with some quick candor: "I've seen you more in the past few months than I saw your predecessor in seven years."

My EQ radar sensed something in the mayor's voice. One cardinal rule of mine is to never criticize those who sat in the chair before me. These jobs are *hard*, and I default to believing people did the best they could. So while outwardly acknowledging the mayor's comment—and recognizing, inside, there was work yet to do—I believed the same of this man. I sensed that he was clearing a path that would lead me to a fuller understanding of the community's priorities.

I repeated this process in each community—meeting with people the college already had some connection with and warming up those relationships. It was familiar ground, but I'd next venture to the unknown.

Cold Calls

I needed to determine which influential community members to consult for further perspective.

Leaning on the college's existing friends for insight and introductions that might help me gain it, I noticed that mayors often introduced me to their administrative staff, most notably their economic development officers. I cultivated relationships with these civil servants because we shared a goal: sustainable community prosperity.

Of course, I did my own research too.

I studied the members of the chambers of commerce boards—business leaders in each community who were invested in their communities' success. Then, I made a point of dropping in—what salespeople refer to as "cold-calling"—at their businesses.

Sometimes I'd connect briefly with the relevant board member; sometimes they were not around. But eventually I'd catch them, and my visibility (and persistence!) laid a foundation of trust. It was another route to the future, as deeper conversations ensued.

Like my economic development friends at city hall, these folks also valued economic sustainability and strived for excellence in their businesses.

Another tool aiding my quest to learn what mattered to my communities was attendance at municipal government meetings—specifically, gatherings of the mayors from every city and town in the region. Their municipalities ranged in population from a few hundred people to tens of thousands, but I learned that their mutual concern was the same: how to attract talent to their communities and reverse the trend of professionals commuting in for work—and right back out at the end of the day.

"We want professionals to be a part of our communities," one of the mayors began. "We want to see them at our town events and pushing their grocery carts on the weekends." The room roared in approval.

This need was further confirmed at a symposium on sustainability at one of the province's research universities.

The event drew community leaders, business owners, educators, researchers, and municipal and provincial government officials. All placed great value on the cornerstone of sustainability, and a value I strongly share: **access to services**. Which of course includes postsecondary education.

Shining a Light

Later discussions consistently confirmed access to services as crucial to every locality. This offered Grasslands the opportunity to act, to help fill the need.

My slogan became "What can we do for you?"

Speaking with a donor or business owner in one of our campus communities, I regularly expressed my gratitude for their long-standing support. "But what," I'd add, "can *we* do for *you*?"

"I'd appreciate speaking to your business students for a few minutes," one replied. "I want to explain to them that this community has options for them—they can make a living here. I'm not sure they recognize that."

We made it so, filling his need.

Another community's commitment to providing services to residents led to an effort to build a public recreation center for volleyball, basketball, indoor soccer, and other events, as space for such activities was limited at the time.

We responded by opening our campus gym for public use, from amateur sports to performing arts events to a range of other community and cultural gatherings. That gym became a beacon—a place for the community to gather and connect—and provided relief for the city's stressed facilities while fundraising for the new building progressed.

Another of our campus communities was isolated—over two hours from the next major center, with a handful of small communities scattered between. Health care was, therefore, a hot topic—in particular, the town's difficulty in attracting and retaining nurses. With support from the provincial government, the town regularly attempted to lure nurses through financial incentives. It worked occasionally, but the recruits rarely stayed.

I knew from our data that students who trained locally were more likely to stay local after graduation. Their reasons varied; perhaps their practicum provided an attractive local professional pathway, or maybe they had established a personal network they valued.

We helped by advocating for and launching a nursing program at that campus. The option for locals to train close to home, plus the ability to draw students to the area to study, made it a winning maneuver. Need identified, need fulfilled.

The more our team thought in terms of "How can we help?" the stronger our brand became.

Another campus struggled with student housing, a key element in attracting nonlocals who might opt to study elsewhere instead of making the long commute. It was a missed opportunity to turn at least a slice of our student body into future, locally based professionals.

We purchased our first student residence in that community, filling another need—and increasing our value proposition to prospective enrollees.

I could go on and on. From small, inexpensive gestures, like opening a gymnasium to the public, to big investments, like creating a whole new program or establishing student housing, identifying and collaborating to fill the needs of our organization's constituents has been a defining factor in Grasslands's success.

> COOPERATION—ROOTED IN VALUES—STRENGTHENS RELATIONSHIPS.

Yet one story moves me the most and is one that, to my mind, helps instill in our youngest people a lifelong valuing of education in general, and of constituent-focused educational institutions specifically.

A First Nations community neighbors one of Grasslands's campuses. This means that, at any one time, our student population is from 75 to 90 percent comprised of people from that Indigenous community.

When Brad's Listening Tour stopped there, the stories were about barriers to our classrooms, the greatest being access to childcare: many of our First Nation students are young parents or responsible for caring for younger family members.

Our response was to take a seat at the leadership table, charged with planning the construction of the town's first licensed daycare center. Next, we initiated an early childhood education program at our campus, building a workforce for that new business.

Working in concert, the college, the town, and most importantly, the First Nations community identified a need, and our collaboration might well transcend generations. I'm already looking forward to seeing kids in the childcare center today as Grasslands's students tomorrow.

Cooperation—rooted in values—strengthens relationships.

Amanda Lea Kaiser writes that working together toward a common goal with shared value creates an intentional relationship that can foster future collaboration.[66]

Community engagement scholars Winston Tinglin and Donna Joyette add, derived from their book *Community Engagement in a Changing Social Landscape*, that in a climate of uncertainty, people are more willing to work together to better the lives of their families and communities.[67]

And as Trey Taylor explains in *CEO Excellence*, the key is finding that one thing that can bring everyone together.[68]

The initiatives I've described did just that: they aligned with the shared values of everyone involved. That wide support made our goals of building community, supporting our host municipalities' priorities, and strengthening relations all around much easier to reach.

Other Perspectives

I've always wondered how other leaders go about discovering their communities' values and discerning constituents' priorities.

One of my former colleagues, a dean of business, created an advisory committee. The group comprised distinguished business leaders and entrepreneurs in the community.

While the intel and advice she received were gold, and group sessions were generally acknowledged as very effective from a time- and resource-management perspective, she acknowledged that the

---

66 Kaiser, A. L. (2023). *Elevating engagement: Uncommon strategies for creating a thriving member community.* PageTwo.

67 Tinglin, W., & Joyette, D. (2020). *Community engagement in a changing social landscape.* FriesenPress.

68 Taylor, T. (2020). *A CEO only does three things.* Board Advisors.

work of managing the committee and its high-profile (and sometimes, high-maintenance) players was *enormous*.

That, for me, is what makes one-on-one conversations between two people who trust each other the gold standard for effective community engagement.

Makara Rumley, an author and environmental justice attorney who has developed community engagement programs for a host of government agencies, agrees. She suggests that having one-on-one conversations with community thought leaders and elected officials is often the best practice.[69]

I received an objective lesson in Rumley's work upon making the incorrect assumption that my community members would want to be part of a college advisory group, like that my aforementioned colleague had formed. The mere *mention* of a new committee or council left people shifting uncomfortably in their seats or, worse, totally turned off. Noticing this, I started trying to salvage the idea: What about a focus group?

My EQ radar sensed the cold front deepening within the group.

Words like "council" or "committee" impart a formality (and signify long meetings, the last thing busy people need more of). Focus groups, meanwhile, allow more extroverted individuals to overtake conversations and bring bias to the discussion, as decades in classrooms—whatever desk I happened to occupy—had taught me.

No, our communities did not value councils, boards, committees, and focus groups. They wanted handshakes and one-on-one dialogue. With trust thus established, people were freed from any sense that they should perhaps soften their take on things and were more prone

---

69   Rumley, M. (2020). *Modern-day strategies for community engagement.* Purposely Created.

to give me what I needed: *their* unvarnished truths, told from *their* points of view.

Other colleagues agreed. One former teammate, now a college president, organized one hundred coffees over her first one hundred days. Another president had one-on-one meetings with *every* employee.

Hard data can aid learning—from strategic plans and employee surveys to financial reports—but management consultant and author Michael D. Watkins encourages us to seek "soft" information as well: to gain intelligence by talking to people who have vital knowledge about your situation.[70]

This is especially valuable in differentiating the external realities from the internal perceptions of folks from the top of the organizational chart to those on the front line, Watkins notes.[71]

History Lessons

Being an avid student of history, I am intrigued not just by the stories it tells and the lessons it teaches us but also by history's tendency to change as our perspectives shift.

Let Prosecutor Brad explain ...

Exhibit A: The brontosaurus was one of Little Brad's favorite dinosaurs. Yet as I reached adolescence, I became disconnected from the world of the extinct "thunder lizard."

When I was a young father, my son followed my early passion for dinosaurs, so imagine my bewilderment—as I reengaged with a world I had not known for decades—at learning that the brontosaurus *did not exist*! I mean, yeah, extinction and all ... but as far as paleontol-

---

70   Watkins, M. D. (2013). *The first 90 days, updated and expanded: Proven strategies for getting up to speed faster and smarter.* Harvard Business Review Press.

71   Ibid.

ogy was concerned, it was now an *apatosaurus*. And *then*, writing this book decades later *still*, I discovered that "brontosaurus" seems to be making a comeback.[72]

Exhibit B: My childhood fascination with outer space also returned via my son's similar passion.

But Little Brad lived on the third of *nine* planets circling the sun, while Brad the Young Father taught his son about *eight* planets, and the debate about what to call the icy celestial object I knew as Pluto still rages.[73]

Exhibit C: My favorite lesson on perspectives comes via bluesman Robert Johnson, whom musicologists and popular writers alike revere.

Paul Guralnick, for example, in his book *Searching for Robert Johnson*, celebrates him and echoes others in calling him the King of the Delta Blues Singers.[74] Yet Elijah Wald suggests a polarizing position, questioning Johnson's legacy—and points out Johnson's plagiarism of other artists of his day.[75]

My closing argument lies in the history of something near and dear to me: the electric guitar.

Considered in its infancy a noisy distraction associated with youthful rebellion, today the electric guitar is celebrated with museum exhibitions honoring seminal players and the companies that made the "axes" they played. The former noisy distractions are now collected,

---

72 Osterloff, E. (2015). *Brontosaurus: Reinstating a prehistoric icon.* National History Museum. Retrieved from https://www.nhm.ac.uk/discover/brontosaurus-reinstating-a-prehistoric-icon.html

73 Alt, E. (2024). *Did Pluto ever actually stop being a planet? Experts debate.* National Geographic. Retrieved from https://www.nationalgeographic.com/science/article/pluto-planet-dwarf-planetoid-solar-system

74 Guralnick, P. (2020). *Searching for Robert Johnson: The life and legend of the King of the Delta Blues Singers.* Hachette UK.

75 Wald, E. (2004). *Escaping the delta: Robert Johnson and the invention of the blues.* Amistad.

traded, and treasured like rare antiques, and their players are celebrated as icons of Western music—some, like Jimi Hendrix, with their own museums.[76]

My point?

As you get to know your constituencies, be prepared for divergent "history" lessons. New information and differing perspectives alter "accepted" history. Musicologist Victor Coelho writes that studies of the past, especially the informal past, may reveal *simultaneous histories existing.*[77]

> IT'S ALL ABOUT PERSPECTIVE, AND ONLY PERSISTENT CURIOSITY PROVIDES A PICTURE OF HISTORY THAT IS FULL ENOUGH TO OFFER GENUINE INSIGHT.

As I spoke with community members, their stories revealed these concurrent histories. I remembered my Gallwey and listened without judgment, respecting their viewpoints, even if details conflicted greatly with other versions I'd heard of the same history. It's all about perspective, and only persistent curiosity provides a picture of history that is full enough to offer genuine insight.

Be Here, Now—Not There, Then

In leading Grasslands College, I often reflect on the board's direction that we innovate—a reasonable goal, one aimed at keeping things current and forward facing.

Yet the honest conversations born of the trust that my visibility created taught me what mattered to *other* stakeholders and exposed gaps between my initial assumptions and the reality on the ground.

---

76   Museum of Popular Culture. (2024). Seattle. Retrieved from https://www.mopop.org/

77   Coelho, V. A. (2003). Picking through cultures: A guitarist's music history. *The Cambridge Companion to the Guitar*, 3–12.

Indeed, I started and ended in two very different places. My initial urge to try fix everything immediately by duplicating what proved successful in other places gave way to learning about *this* place—and a realization: I was being driven by the wrong desires.

Early in this chapter, I recounted how, at Protest U, my success was greeted with press and community attention, making me something of a local celebrity. (Perhaps it was because I never became famous as a musician, but whatever the reason, I must admit that the experience had also made me a bit of a press monster!)

But at Grasslands, the initiatives simply identified and fulfilled community values. They were not showy or sexy, and they did not garner national headlines, but they mattered to the communities they impacted. That was paramount.

Discovering those communities' values shaped my approach to engagement here. I directed programming and partnerships toward what our communities needed, unconcerned with making the news. Filling those needs without the fullest possible understanding of what each community valued—and why—would never have worked.

Maybe I wouldn't win an innovation award at Grasslands, but serving the communities' values was far more rewarding. Finding alignment between my own values and those of the college and its constituents helped me discover the pathway to deliberate conversations about partnerships—a practice we will examine fully in chapter 6.

Closing Thoughts

Understanding your community's priorities and discovering its values is critical.

Local partners and influential community members can provide perspectives, which produce insight. Consult them often, using direct conversations to uncover passionate interests. These discussions will illuminate what resonates locally. And whatever you do, **avoid making assumptions**.

Learn instead, through independent research, observation, asking questions, and listening.

Every interaction I have helps me understand what my community is passionate about and what its priorities are. This helps me see how the college can best serve the community in helping it meet those priorities.

> WHETHER YOU ARE NEW TO A COMMUNITY OR TO A ROLE, REMEMBER: YOU BRING FRESH EYES.

Gathering this vital intel required me to develop the most important skill in cultivating collaboration. As Reeves, Frey, and Fisher put it: *listen—* just listen and become comfortable with silence and contemplation, instead of giving in to the urge to fill moments best filled with silent contemplation rather than with more talking.[78]

Whether you are new to a community or to a role, remember: you bring fresh eyes.

Therefore, use them! Attend events and observe. Build connections through conversation. Be curious and genuinely interested. Ask questions. Listen. Reframe what you have heard and reflect it back, to ensure that you fully understand.

Then, plainly state that you want to know how your organization can best serve the community.

---

78   Reeves, D., Frey, N., & Fisher, D. (2022). *Confronting the crisis of engagement: Creating focus and resilience for students, staff, and communities.* Corwin Press.

Key Takeaways

This chapter explored strategies for researching what most matters to the community your organization serves, in order to inform engagement.

- Effective research avoids assumptions.

- Identify your community's values and priorities by gathering multiple perspectives.

- Consult partners, monitor media, and collect data.

- Ask community partners the question: "What can *we* do for *you*?"

For Reflection

Think about the one-on-one conversations that have most profoundly impacted your life. What did they have in common? What made them so impactful? Can you recreate that sense of trust and intimate sharing with your constituents? How? (Hint: It starts with a handshake.)

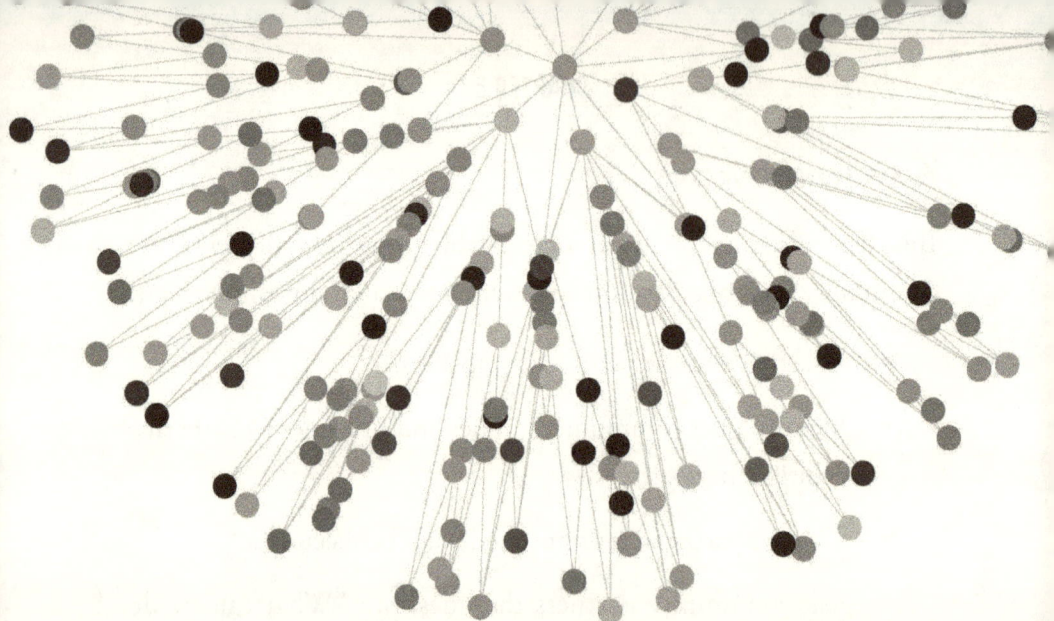

CHAPTER 6

IDENTIFY YOUR POTENTIAL PARTNERS

Partnership is not a legal contract between two individuals. It's an emotional alliance between two people who are committed to each other's success.

—WARREN BUFFETT[79]

In chapter 2, I shared reflections about my time as director at Protest U and finding my voice.

I had inherited an unhappy group, upset in part about the dean's decisions, which ultimately led to a high-profile public protest on the steps of the new concert hall. The waters eventually calmed in my department, but a larger storm was brewing.

Rumors began circulating that Protest U was about to "blow up" our faculty (which entailed legally dissolving the business unit by

---

79   Buffett, W. E. (2021). *The essays of Warren Buffett: Lessons for corporate America.* Cardozo Law Review.

eliminating the programs and laying off staff). Enrollments had been declining for years, and finances were a growing concern. Adding to the suspicion, Dean Donald was increasingly absent from campus, taking extended time away for minor medical procedures. The rumor mill spun out a story that he was having the work done while he still had health benefits.

I stayed visible and kept my ear to the ground. I leaned into my good relations with colleagues and gathered intel from my spies. To understand the threat and think strategically, I needed to learn all I could, without adding to the mounting tales across campus or the tension within our faculty.

Then it happened: the summoning.

I was called to the vice president's office. The end-of-day meeting time made me curious and a bit uneasy, and on my way, I reflected on the past few months.

The department I was leading existed within that struggling faculty. My research determined the threat was real, so I started planning. I met with some of the university's deans. Perhaps one of them would adopt my music department, saving us from the impending explosion.

"*Arts* exists within *performing arts*," I told the dean of arts. He said he'd get back to me. "Music *is* a science," I insisted to the dean of science. No sale. I even met with the dean of health, outlining music's physical demands on the body.

Admittedly, it was not my best work.

Perhaps my sales pitches ruffled feathers? I reran the conversations in my head as I waited outside the VP's office.

An hour later, I walked back across campus toward the performing arts building. My assumptions were wrong. It wasn't a reprimand, but an offer to lead the faculty as interim dean, replacing Dean Donald, and I would keep my director gig too.

Funny. I entered that office fully anticipating a scolding—at least—and emerged instead with a second job! Should I celebrate? It was a lot to process.

Today, the experience provides a lasting memory of impostor syndrome, a condition that seemed to linger always. I returned to my office somewhat stunned, opened my internet browser, and searched "how to be a dean."

As my mind settled, the feelings of surprise and fakery—my own—faded. Just one distinct feeling remained: loneliness.

The Lone Ranger

As a child of the 1970s, I remember consuming reruns of the classic 1950s television series *The Lone Ranger*, starring Clayton Moore.[80] I was a superfan; I had the hat, the plastic gun, and the iconic black mask. (Living in my city's suburbs, I concluded that asking my parents for a horse would likely prove futile.) Except for his trusted companion Tonto (played by Jay Silverheels), the Lone Ranger's life was one of solitude.

Now I knew how he felt.

In my new interim dean role, I experienced the sense of isolation that has led leaders down through time to affirm the old adage "It's lonely at the top."

Later in my career, I would enjoy and lean into a network of colleagues and other leaders I could confide in, easing what I now felt. But still rising through the ranks, I had not yet built that group. John C. Maxwell, one of the most read and respected leadership authors, writes that the loneliness at the top is real. All the more reason, he

---

80 Striker, F., & Trendle, G. W. (1949–1957). *The Lone Ranger.* ABC Television Network.

says, for a leader to understand *why* they are there.[81] And I didn't yet understand why the vice president had put me in the role.

At Protest U, Dean Donald's unpopular decisions prompted the performing arts community to rebel. The protests included faculty, staff, students, partners, donors, and community members rallying together on the steps of the concert hall. They were the culmination of months of turbulence within the department.

Protest U was again needing to make difficult decisions, many of which *I* would now implement. There were signs that more change was coming: canceled programs, reduced staff, receding resources, and rumors of the faculty's imminent death. Yet I neither saw nor sensed any turbulence—no tips of an impending uprising. The only thing worse than the faculty being on the "chopping block" was that no one seemed to care. It was proof of a sparse network, a limited support system—in short, zero community engagement.

The faculty's isolation was real; some even seemed to be *hoping* for its demise. Research might uncover when the faculty *had* been successful, which seemed like a good place to start. So I studied my new faculty, with a focus on its history.

Super Friends

When Little Brad wasn't watching *The Lone Ranger*, he was engaged in reruns of *Adventures of Superman*, starring George Reeves,[82] and *Batman*, starring Adam West.[83] Yet no childhood show impacted me

---

81 Maxwell, J. C. (2007). *The 21 indispensable qualities of a leader: Becoming the person others will want to follow.* HarperCollins Leadership.

82 Siegel, J., & Shuster, J. (1952–1958). *The Adventures of Superman.* Kellogg's.

83 Dozier, W. (1966–1968). *Batman.* ABC Television Network.

CHAPTER 6

like *Super Friends*, based on DC Comics' *Justice League of America*. The show anchored ABC TV's classic Saturday morning cartoon lineup.[84]

The program featured many of pop culture's best-known super-heroes: Batman, Wonder Woman, Aquaman, and Superman. Each crime fighter was well known in their own right, but *Super Friends* united them, creating a formidable partnership that pursued their shared values of truth and justice. It was a classic example of the partnership equation of one plus one equals three, where partnering makes the new team greater than the sum of its parts.

As I studied my struggling faculty, I learned that partnerships, on- and off-campus, had once been a touchstone. Further research showed that many of our historic alliances had become dormant. I wondered about the differences between the music department I directed and my new, broader portfolio. Why such a difference in the community's response to the university's hard decisions?

The music department's community engagement was strong. Thanks, in part, to partnerships with many professional and amateur arts organizations across the city, its community roots had grown wide and deep. In short, the music program had friends.

My new faculty ... *mmm, not so much*. We needed to reengage the community.

This excited me, because it also aligned with *my* values.

My evolving professional experience provided me confidence in my leadership skills and belief in my ability to transfer success, but doing so required ignoring my Self 1's efforts to pollute my thoughts. I had experience, and more importantly, success, engaging the community and believed we could do it again here. In other words, I was starting to understand my *why*.

---

84 Gardener, F. (1973–1985). *Super Friends*. DC Comics, Hanna-Barbera Productions, & Warner Brothers Television.

287

Further study revealed that at one time, our programming aligned more directly with industry trends, making sector partners easy to find. But the regional economy had been transforming, and our disengagement from the community had left us lacking. We had become disconnected from the community we were supposed to be serving. We needed to realign our program offerings, and quickly. But how?

Enter our Super Friends.

Weed 101

Medicinal cannabis had been legal in Canada for several years, but now the federal government was planning to broaden the law to include recreational use, creating commercial possibilities. This emerging sector required a workforce, so I wondered if our faculty could take a leadership role in cannabis education.

Of course, my idea meant enduring my colleagues' friendly jokes.

One day during Deans Council (a regular gathering of each faculty's top administrators), another dean teased me, "Will you be serving Popsicles in class in case students get the munchies?" Another chimed in, "This [a cannabis program] is what happens when you put a musician in charge of a faculty." We all laughed, and they were highly (heh) supportive—but jokes aside, community was clearly building at the executive level.

Externally, I made myself visible and connected with the companies in the medicinal cannabis market that were planning to go commercial. There was sure to be a massive consumer market.

"We had 50 staff last year, and we're up to 100 this year," one local CEO told me. "By Christmas, I'll need 250 employees and 500 by this time next year. There's no ceiling." I continued hearing similar stories and saw our North Star.

This emerging sector required a workforce. We would respond by providing education and training. However, we needed a partner; our school was unknown in this sector.

Back to research, where I learned that due to its relative youth, the sector's few educational offerings seemed focused on two key areas: production (how to grow better plants efficiently) and legislation—understanding the new laws.

We connected with a university that had pioneered a cannabis education program. Located in British Columbia and known in cannabis circles as the home of "BC Bud," it was a perfect match; the school's geographic location and pop culture tag could enhance our own credibility. I'll call this school Green Leaf U.

Finding Shared Values

David led Green Leaf U's large cannabis education program. At about three years old, it was well developed, and with cannabis becoming fully legal, David and his team wanted to expand the reach of their curriculum.

We at Protest U had zero experience with cannabis or related agricultural-science programs. We may have lacked street cred on that front, but our university had a strong regional brand and was well recognized in other areas. David and I saw the partnership's potential for leveraging Protest U's local brand awareness with his BC Bud subject matter expertise.

We sent many emails back and forth. His response time was quick, and though it was only through email, I felt like we connected.

Then it happened: he suggested we meet. *What would I wear?* Would this newfound connection feel the same in person? I was admittedly, and somewhat surprisingly, nervous.

We met for breakfast at a trendy restaurant in a hip part of town, and my concerns melted; the chemistry was immediate. After an hour of talking and eating, we realized we hadn't talked business at all. Too late; it was time to go!

I spent the morning parading David around campus, showing him our facilities, and introducing him to my team, our staff, and other important stakeholders. We even had a short sit-down with my boss, the VP. David was deeply engaged in every conversation.

Lunch was as easy as breakfast, and before we knew it, the afternoon had slipped away too! It was time to walk David to his rental car and send him back to the airport.

What strikes me most when reflecting on that day is how little we discussed the program, contracts, or other "nuts-and-bolts" details. Instead, we shared stories that revealed our values. We got acquainted. I heard his voice and saw his vision. We had a partner, and I had a friend. I wasn't alone.

> **BY PROVIDING ACCESS TO EDUCATION, WE CREATED PATHWAYS TO EMPLOYMENT.**

We moved forward, signed the papers, and launched the joint (heh) program.

And it worked.

Our recognized partner in Green Leaf U gave us the street cred we lacked in the sector. The Protest U campus community fully embraced the opportunity, as did the economic sector. By providing access to education, we created pathways to employment, which only increased our value proposition to the community we served. The learners came. Classes were full, then wait-listed.

The movie was a hit. *But could I produce a worthy sequel?*

Building a Blueprint

We took the same approach with other emerging workforce trends, particularly in information technology, another area we were not known for. We partnered with High Tech U and were suddenly offering tech programs. Once again, our strong regional brand, combined with our partner's subject matter credibility, created a formidable collaboration.

We continued to partner with other schools, creating a full roster of Super Friends.

The successes garnered significant media attention and illuminated what we did beyond these new, novel programs. But the innovative partnerships were turning the ship, and our new friendships alleviated my loneliness. Our network was growing, and I researched additional regional, national, and international organizations to connect with. I attended conferences and events, following what by now was my go-to practice.

I showed up for visibility, participated by giving presentations, sponsored conferences and events, and finally, joined committees and boards, so I'd have a hand in the planning processes. Through these steps I connected, and thanks to our successes, we no longer went looking for partnership opportunities; *they* came looking for *us*.

We now had some tough choices to make but made them easier by choosing to foster the collaborations that were most likely to mutually benefit both partners.

Symbiosis

One summer, Little Brad's family ventured the roughly one-million-mile journey by station wagon from Alberta to California. (Maybe I've exaggerated the distance, but to Little Brad, it felt that long.)

A highlight was our visit to Universal Studios to see the set of the movie *Jaws*.[85]

As we approached, my heart pounded. Sharks are terrifying to many. As a child, I even had anxiety swimming in the deep end of the public pool. Getting closer to the exhibit, we noticed a sign: "Closed for Maintenance." Then we saw it: the massive mechanical shark sat on solid ground, out of the water, awaiting repairs. I was disappointed but a little relieved too.

Yet my fear fueled an interest in learning more about these apex predators.

I learned of a fascinating partnership between great white sharks and pilot fish. The pilot fish gains protection from predators—the shark, from parasites. It's the definition of a win-win, symbiotic partnership. And it was exactly the model we followed when seeking partnerships.

Harvard Business School's James Austin writes about the importance of knowing for yourself what you want from a partnership—and not just what you are looking for, but also how you will measure success and what metrics you will use.[86]

Sure, we investigated each school's reputation—Green Leaf U, High Tech U, and others. But so many strong brands existed, we found that investigating prospective partners' missions and definitions of success helped us *best* understand if we'd found a good fit.

When a prospect approached us, got down on one knee, and popped the question, we didn't consider their looks, zodiac signs, or whether they liked long walks on the beach. We wanted to know their values.

---

85   Spielberg, S. (1975). *Jaws.* Universal Pictures.

86   Austin, J. E. (2000). Strategic collaboration between nonprofits and businesses. *Nonprofit and Voluntary Sector Quarterly, 29*(1_suppl), 69–97.

Aligning Values

Teenage Brad worked at a music store, teaching guitar and doing some retail sales. When the store was slow, I'd read the bulletin board, the closest thing in the 1980s to social media.

The store's community bulletin board always had posters advertising bands' upcoming shows and other events. It also featured classified ads, whether by people selling gear or looking to join a band. In our store, and across the performance universe, musicians cited their influences when seeking band auditions.

In 1981, Lars Ulrich placed an ad in *The Recycler*, a Newport Beach, California, newspaper, that read: "Drummer looking for other metal musicians to jam with Tigers of Pan Tang, Diamond Head, and Iron Maiden."[87] James Hetfield responded, and Metallica was born. It might never have happened without Ulrich's list of influential artists because it spoke to who he was as a musician and the genre of music he wanted to work in. It's no exaggeration to say that list was the most important part of the ad.

Likewise, we at Protest U, when considering partner organizations, investigated what influenced *them*. Who *were* they? What did they stand for? Did our respective missions, vision, and values align?

Survival Skills

Regardless of my professional experience, I didn't make my children take music lessons. Instead, we encouraged them to explore and find the things that interested them. However, there *was* one nonnegotiable: they had to take swimming lessons. Doing so might one day

---

87   RIP Magazine. (2024). Retrieved from https://www.ripmagazine.com/

save their life, or someone else's. Swimming was a life skill they had to have.

In my world of publicly funded postsecondary education, I think of building synergetic partnerships in the same way: as a life skill necessary for survival.

Erica Yamamura and Kent Koth, community engagement thought leaders at Seattle University, write that partnerships can mutually benefit the participants, which allows postsecondaries and the communities they serve to maximize resources that reveal mutual benefits and yield big and lasting social change.[88] In an age when governments are pressuring publicly funded entities to find alternative revenue streams and resources, building economies of scale and leveraging collective intelligence is, with increasing frequency, the difference between scaling back services and multiplying them.

This is why I continue researching partnership models and best practices. Broader knowledge takes me beyond my lived experience, opening my eyes to new options and approaches. Through all my research and lived experiences, one thing is for sure: you *must* communicate, and often.

Yamamura and Koth write about temperature checks—the importance of regularly connecting with partners to understand what's working well and what needs adjusting, especially getting in front of any problems before they get out of hand.[89]

David from Green Leaf U stayed connected with me, and I checked in with him regularly. At Protest U, our reputation as a partner of choice grew out of strong communication that emphasized

---

88   Yamamura, E. K., & Koth, K. (2018). *Place-based community engagement in higher education: A strategy to transform universities and communities.* Routledge.

89   Ibid.

taking our partners' success and satisfaction with our collaboration at least as seriously as we took our own.

Closing Thoughts

Partnerships are essential to progress and foundational to your professional network and support system. Explore your community to identify potential partners and proactively build partnerships.

Seek out the organizations and influencers in your area with shared values and alignment on priorities and passions. Leverage your network to connect, create introductions, and initiate potential partnerships. Your primary goal? Mutually beneficial collaborations: partnerships where both sides benefit.

The process can feel a bit like finding your way to the bathroom in the middle of the night with no lights on. Slowly and cautiously, you sense your way forward, hoping not to stub your toe—or worse. Building successful partnerships is similar. Follow the best advice you can find, but have your EQ radar on at all times so you're certain to remain aware and responsive.

Seeking synergetic relationships with industry, community groups, other postsecondary institutions, arts organizations, and government has been my passion. Building such partnerships has been a cornerstone of my tenures at various institutions. Through deep community engagement, I aim to continually embed our good work into the region's fabric.

To become a partner of choice, make your business's brand attractive to your prospective collaborators. Demonstrate your brand's value. Show how the places where your passions align will enhance

REMEMBER THAT PEOPLE WILL WANT TO WORK WITH YOUR ORGANIZATION—OR NOT—BECAUSE OF *YOU*—ITS LEADER.

your partner's brand and community standing and be ready to share the benefits that you're hoping to see from the collaboration too.

Finally, remember that people will want to work with your organization—or not—because of *you*—its leader. You are the face of your organization, and the culture you create contributes—for good or ill, your choice—to its appeal to potential partners.

Key Takeaways

This chapter explored strategies for finding partners and collaborators for mutual benefit.

- Partnerships create possibilities.

- Recognize potential allies with shared values by identifying the mutual benefits you and they hope to derive.

- Propose win-win collaborations.

For Reflection

Make a list of the traits your ideal partner will possess—what are you looking for? What are your deal-breakers?

Identify up to five potential partners in your community by researching your shared priorities. Then reach out to set up introductory meetings.

CHAPTER 7

PUT OUT THE WELCOME MAT

One of the marvelous things about community is that it enables us to welcome and help people in a way we couldn't as individuals.

—JEAN VANIER[90]

My tenure as president of Grasslands College began on August 1.

Exploring my new campus felt at times like being in an episode of *The Walking Dead*, a horror-drama set in a postapocalyptic Earth with limited life.[91] That's not to suggest my new colleagues were zombies, but that the lifeless spaces on campus seemed to outnumber the more vibrant, lively ones.

"Where are all the people?" I thought.

Granted, it was still summer, when things are quieter in the education sector. Still, in past roles, I prioritized opening campus

---

90   Vanier, J. (1989). *Community and growth*. Paulist Press.

91   Darabont, F. (2010). *The walking dead*. Idiot Box Productions.

spaces for community use, *especially* at off-peak times. Summer workshops, youth day camps, and professional development offerings were the lowest-hanging fruit: they were valued by the communities and industry partners we served, and cost-efficient for them *and* us, because there's a point when an institution's emptiness becomes unhealthy, whatever the season.

I soon learned that we offered no postsecondary summer classes. It wasn't until mid-August that we would see more faculty and staff on campus, preparing for our students' return. September marked the time the hallways once again hummed with the vibrancy I'd been waiting for.

Even then, however, our campus only stirred during business hours. There was little evening or weekend activity. The gymnasium, which included a performing arts stage, was booked just 3 percent of its available time.

The underusage bothered me. Empty spaces are lost opportunities for community connection, openness, and inclusion at the school.

Being visible in the community is necessary, but seeing the community in *our* spaces is equally important. We had to enable access and open our relationship with the public, and facilitating community events was one way to do this.

We needed to put out our welcome mat.

Making an Investment

As my professional journey progressed, my program portfolios changed, yet the similarities at each destination persisted.

I regularly inherited struggling organizations clinging to aged ideals, notably that postsecondaries are exclusive "ivory towers." I countered this thinking by using our spaces to support public events that aligned with our values, complemented our programming, and created external engagement. It was an investment in our community.

In chapter 3, I talked about the Haunted Hall at Faraway U. We opened the doors to our historic venue and became inclusive, which led to our classrooms and rehearsal spaces following suit. We hosted community arts organizations and other related events, which complemented our core business of arts programming. The campus buzzed with activity. Ultimately, we became an arts beacon, which aided business success, both ours and our partners'.

In my director-plus-dean role at Protest U, I used our spaces to host major events, including an international piano competition, a cannabis conference, an e-sports tournament, and a tech symposium. And as diverse as those events might sound, each shared a connection to our program offerings.

We also hosted the Women in Business Awards, Pride events, Indigenous celebrations, multicultural gatherings, and any other activity that aligned with our values and affirmed the inclusiveness of our campus. Saying this helped fill our hallways and spaces is an understatement: we had become a part of the community, so of course, our students, employees, and partners looked like the community we served.

Welcoming complementary community groups into our spaces, we channeled our inner *Battlestar Galactica*. Again, our welcome mat went out, and engagement increased, again aiding business success.

In my newest role at Grasslands College, the mandate was to provide education to fulfill labor market demand. While our programs addressed this mission, our business was struggling, and our spaces were exclusive rather than inclusive. As part of the solution, we needed to broaden our external engagement and invest in our community.

Getting Started

Earlier in my leadership career, I had a favorite coffee shop on campus. In fact, I held several meetings there every day. People joked that my regular booth was my second office.

Ryan ran the coffee shop. He appreciated the support, and I appreciated him for many reasons, including his delicious beverages. Ryan's place created an optimal atmosphere for doing business.

One day, Ryan surprised me with an invitation to the launch of his newest location, an off-campus venture downtown. "Wonderful, and congratulations!" I said. "I'll be there."

The next week, I arrived at Ryan's launch. As I entered, I was again surprised, this time by the somewhat sparse crowd. It reminded me that I hadn't seen much publicity or advertising for the event.

Ryan greeted me; he was beaming. I could tell he was pleased.

He explained that this was his "soft launch," with invited guests being his most loyal customers, close friends, and some family. "We wanted to start with our supporters and work out the bugs before bringing in the strangers."

Ryan's soft launch inspired me to apply a similar strategy in opening our postsecondary spaces to the community. We didn't create social media posts or take out ads in local media sources; rather, we quietly vocalized our intention to those already closest to us—current supporters, including staff and existing partners. Like Ryan, this allowed us to work out our bugs before we opened our doors to everyone. After all, our core business was delivering education and training to meet labor market demands, not facility rentals or event planning. We had processes and policies to create, and we needed some practice events too.

We started with our boardroom.

The first was Janice.

She was on the board of a local nonprofit group that fundraised and provided underprivileged youth with access to recreational sports, by supplying equipment and covering registration costs for qualifying families. Its values alignment with ours—enabling access—was powerful, so we opened our boardroom to Janice's group for its monthly meetings.

Next was Leonard, who sat on the city's public library board. The library and the college had multiple value alignments, making it a rather obvious fit. A few logistical conversations later, they, too, were meeting in our boardroom.

Isabella, meanwhile, was on the board of the community's newcomer welcome center, whose clients often enrolled in our English Language Program. We put Isabella's board on the schedule, and as other "friends" came forward, we followed a similar process; the room was occupied a few evenings each week.

It was a good start.

Next, we opened our gymnasium.

Some of our employees were involved with the soccer association and volleyball club. Soon, recreational youth indoor soccer and volleyball were being played on evenings and weekends.

These activities allowed us to stealthily serve these groups while working out any kinks on our end. With our soft launch a success, we opened wider.

As the buzz grew organically within the community, more people came forward.

Word spread that our doors were open and ready to serve our community. We continued by connecting with organizations and businesses that aligned with our values and complemented our programs.

Our gym's full stage attracted concerts, plays, and other arts productions. I smiled seeing an advertisement for a concert to be held at the *Grasslands College Theater*. "Theater" seemed like a bit of an advertising exaggeration, but then again, to the users, the gym *was* a theater.

In time, multicultural groups approached us. We strongly value diversity and expanded the schedule to stage events exploring our First Nations' history and celebrating the various ethnicities in our region. These events allowed the community to learn, interact, and experience things from new perspectives.

Thanks to honing our skills on one-off events, we next sought ways to make certain offerings occur regularly. Often, the goal was predictability, so people would connect a given time of year with a recurring event. As the months went by, we identified and sought out events that we wanted to be associated, in the public's mind, with the college.

FROM BEING VISIBLE AND PARTICIPATING ...

Like our strategy of engaging the community at external events, internal activities followed a similar trajectory. As noted in chapter 4, it is first about volume and visibility.

Inviting visitors to campus proved to be a great way to connect without the windshield time, and an added opportunity to support our community partners. I'd pop in and say a quick "hello" to parents watching an indoor soccer practice. I'd attend selected performing arts events, which reliably draw a diverse crowd, a cross-section of the city's business and arts community.

... TO COLLABORATION AND SPONSORSHIP

As time has passed, we've become increasingly strategic about our community usage, and our role as partners and sponsors. Hosting chamber of commerce events increases my understanding and awareness of various sectors' needs. It also allows me to share our value proposition with business leaders.

A local high school used our space for its semester-ending business-case competition. I jumped at their invitation to judge and provide opening remarks, which allowed me to share our value proposition with their students—our prospective customers. This is but one example; we continue partnering with external organizations more deliberately, providing us a platform from which we can share our story.

Alternate Capital

A friend once advised me to think of my business like an airplane: "Brad, it's only making money when it's in the air," he said.

I have often transposed that advice to busy hallways, classrooms, and other spaces in the institutions I have served. Yet busy spaces are not always about seeing an immediate return in revenue, as is the case in an airplane with every seat sold. Other types of capital and positive returns accrue to institutions that invest in their communities.

I often refer to my Haunted Hall experience at Faraway U, because it was my first opportunity to control access to school facilities. When we opened the doors of our historic hall and performing arts building, making ancillary revenue was the furthest thing from our minds. We wanted *publicity*.

So we'd ask organizations to put Faraway U's logo on promotional materials, websites, and social media (linked, of course, to our home page). We'd ask them to refer to us as a "friend." It's an approach from which I've never strayed, because it works.

At least to me, postsecondaries fundamentally exist to serve their communities. It's been a staple throughout my career, a value I'm not willing to compromise on. I put out the welcome mat in principle, but as we'll talk about more in part 3, I've also developed a leadership style—a welcoming voice—that reliably encourages consensus and employee buy-in.

Making this approach work requires transparency about *why* we're doing it. Over the years, I've had to explain my strategy to more than a few bean counters whose first language is "spreadsheet"—a vocabulary that only speaks to immediately measurable and quantifiable impacts to the bottom line.

"It's a different type of capital," I explain. "We are investing in our community and reaping the returns through brand recognition, reputation enhancement, and fostering goodwill." By the time I told them about cultivating a small army of community stewards—brand ambassadors whose promotion and advocacy ultimately increased our bottom line—they had either seen the light, or I'd succeeded in making their eyes glaze over. I've never been quite sure which.

I've had some fun at the expense of spreadsheet speakers, but with no offense intended—because they're not alone. People from across your organization are likely to need some onboarding when it comes to the benefits of opening facilities too.

Some may dislike the increased on-campus traffic. Others may wonder why resources are being directed to support activities that seem ancillary to the core mission.

Explaining the *why* is the surest way to build employee buy-in, and building that buy-in is not an option: the last thing you want is for visitors to accept your open-armed invitation to join the campus community, only to get the cold shoulder from staff on their arrival.

So your next objective is clear: building an organizational culture committed to positive community engagement, another task we'll break down in part 3.

Goodwill Equals Growth

"A community room?" I asked.

My surprise and curiosity aroused as Sandy continued.

"We were looking for ways to increase brand awareness, and bringing visitors and nonacademic users to campus was identified as a strategy." She explained that her college's senior leadership had exclusively designated one of its classrooms for community use, free of charge.

It was a welcoming, inclusive environment and resulted in a full calendar of campus activities: community and nonprofit board meetings and annual general meetings, management meetings and retreats of local businesses, community forums, and so on.

Sandy reported that the foot traffic on her campus was remarkable. Further, the advertising these groups did—which included incorporating the college's logo into all promotional materials, plus the local media that occasionally attended the events—compounded the college's visibility in the community *just by opening its doors.*

Remember my waiter and nurse-in-training, Janna, from chapter 1? Just as accessibility to college programs by all interested students drives what I do each day, I know that attracting those students requires visibility and participation in the broader community.

Busy spaces are always good things. They mean that people feel welcome and integrated in your corner of the community, whether it's a retail business selling tangible products or a marketplace of ideas. Anything you do to draw the community in and foster inclusivity will reap positive rewards.

In one of my former haunts, the college had a robust summer day camp program for children and youth called College Kids. Students—as young as four years old—were given an ID number, which was theirs *forever.* When we started pulling data, the results were interesting.

In the prior twenty years, 9 percent of College Kids participants entered one of our postsecondary programs. *Was that a good number?*

We reflected. We didn't have a target, but it was a start, so we began tracking the progress of these young students to understand if there was a pathway from recreational engagement to eventual post-secondary studies.

Why does this matter?

Because customers have choices.

THE GOAL IS FOR THE PUBLIC TO SEE YOUR BUSINESS AS A COMMUNITY ASSET.

My lived experience has connected the dots between community engagement and business success. But acknowledging that my world is not necessarily *the* world, I've gone to the proverbial video tape and explored literature, case studies, and other writings that bear out the success of this model.

The writers and consultants connecting community engagement with business success abound, and their numbers are growing. They all see—many firsthand like me—that fostering spaces for gathering helps to turn your community visitors into brand ambassadors;[92] that an organization's economic success is linked to its social capital, which increases as a result of prioritizing social responsibility, including its community engagement;[93] that social capital is built when an organization and its community understand and address shared needs and goals, which also builds trust;[94] and that community involvement is connected to business success, as these activities help raise an organization's public profile and contribute to building corporate culture (more in part 3).[95]

The goal is for the public to see your business as a community asset. In our case, the college was.

As the *Chronicle of Higher Education*'s Karen Fischer writes, college leaders are prioritizing community relations—hosting cultural events that enrich communities, working with local businesses, public schools, and business entities like the chamber of commerce and

92 Forbes Expert Council (2022). 10 tips for building a positive community around your business. *Forbes.* Retrieved from https://www.forbes.com/sites/theyec/2022/11/08/10-tips-for-building-a-positive-community-around-your-business/?sh=9aa752b42678

93 Rudito, B., Famiola, M., & Anggahegari, P. (2022). Corporate social responsibility and social capital: Journey of community engagement toward community empowerment program in developing country. *Sustainability, 15*(1), 466.

94 Ramírez, R., Aitkin, H., Kora, G., & Richardson, D. (2005). Community engagement, performance measurement, and sustainability: Experiences from Canadian community-based networks.

95 Timmes, M. (2023). *Why community involvement supports business success.* Forbes. Retrieved from https://www.forbes.com/sites/forbescoachescouncil/2023/07/11/why-community-involvement-supports-business-success/?sh=7dc4666a22fc

economic development officers—to help boost public trust and confidence in their institutions.[96]

Skeptical? My very best advice is to track it. Study the metrics before your engagement changes and continue to watch them as you journey through the process and your organization or business evolves. Use the data to tell your story.

Dave's House

A distinct childhood memory is hanging out at Dave's house. His home didn't just have a basement; it had a *lower* basement, too. The basement was the first level below ground, with windows up near the ceiling—typical, right?

But the lower basement was the next floor down, with no windows, and likely not even approaching code these days.

Little Brad and his friends were *terrified* of Dave's lower basement because of its blackness. With the door closed, you couldn't see a hand in front of your face. My friends and I would dare each other and see who could sit in the space longest, alone in the dark, listening to the song "Revolution 9," by the Beatles, before "breaking."[97]

Teenage Brad and his friends *loved* Dave's lower basement because it was almost soundproof. We could play music as loud as we liked and do all sorts of things his parents couldn't hear us doing. It became our hangout of choice. Yet we weren't always sure the space was available.

Dave's older sister hosted friends there, and Dave's parents had their friends and work colleagues over too. The place was a real hub of social activity!

---

96   Fischer, K. (July 2023). College as public good. *Chronicle of High Education.*

97   Lennon, J., & McCartney, P. (1968). *The White Album.* Apple Records.

While Dave's house had some strategic design advantages, the real appeal was how we all *felt* when we were there. Dave's parents were warm and generous, and the apples didn't fall far from the tree: Dave and his sister were also five-star hosts. It was not unusual to approach Dave's house, see the density of parked cars increase, and observe bikes scattered on the front lawn. People wanted to be there because they felt welcome.

Over time, President Brad saw a similar vibe take hold at Grasslands.

The route home each evening assured a campus tour; I navigated what were largely one-way streets. As the months passed, I noticed that the parking lot closest to the gymnasium was usually full, as was the adjacent street parking.

There was so much activity, both after hours and on weekends, that I began struggling to remember the schedule—but that was OK. Knowing our campus had become a gathering place for the community was enough.

One event prompted a type of reflection I wasn't expecting.

I received a text message from an employee on a Saturday morning. "Are you going to Gerald's dad's memorial today?" My EQ radar went on full alert, and my stomach churned.

Gerald was one of our beloved faculty members—long-serving, dedicated to his students, collaborative with staff, connected to businesses, and respected in the community. His dad had died suddenly a few months earlier. We rallied to support him, especially in the immediate days and weeks after the tragedy, but with the passage of time, people go back to their lives.

I wasn't aware of the memorial. The colleague who texted me followed up with a screenshot of Gerald's social media post. His dad's memorial was that afternoon, *at the college gym.*

I arrived on campus a few minutes before the service started, signed the guest book, and sat in the back row. Throughout, my thoughts alternated between absorbing the tributes and appreciating the life of a man I'd never met, while reflecting on the idea of our college as a community space.

Yes, our core business was delivering education and training to meet labor market demand, but serving our communities was a mission I saw more broadly: we provided our stakeholders and constituents with multiple ways to engage our organization, making its relevance in the community further reaching.

We didn't open our spaces to make money. When we charged a fee at all, it covered basic maintenance and renewal costs. Rather, we were investing in our community, and among the returns was one that defies valuation: the growth of a network of strong external supporters.

Closing Thoughts

How can we optimize our business's reputation in the community to affect consumers' decisions?

In my world, those consumers are prospective students because, to be clear, students are *customers*. They have choices as to where they spend their money, and my job is to ensure that we are in the running. To do so, we must have a recognized, reputable, and trusted brand in the community.

YOUR EFFORTS TO BECOME MORE WELCOMING WILL ORGANICALLY GROW ENGAGEMENT, GOODWILL, AND LASTING IMPACTS IN YOUR COMMUNITY.

Openness and access are the objectives. Reach them by establishing new ways to open up to your community, such as hosting events, partnering with local groups to cosponsor activities, collaborating with other organizations on events and programs, and offering resources without expectation of payment.

Contribute space and services, and redirect funds freely. Your efforts to become more welcoming will organically grow engagement, goodwill, and lasting impacts in your community.

Here in part 2, I've mostly referred to "community" in the phrase "community engagement" as the *external* community. But it is equally important to engage our internal community: our employees. We'll focus on doing so in part 3.

Key Takeaways

This chapter explored the power of creating inclusive spaces and events to bring your community together. Remember:

- An open front door invites people in.

- Provide access to facilities.

- Host inclusive events.

- Partner with community groups.

- Give resources freely.

- When we create welcoming spaces, engagement follows.

For Reflection

Audit your organization's current accessibility, events, partnerships, and resource sharing. Identify up to five steps to help make your organization more welcoming.

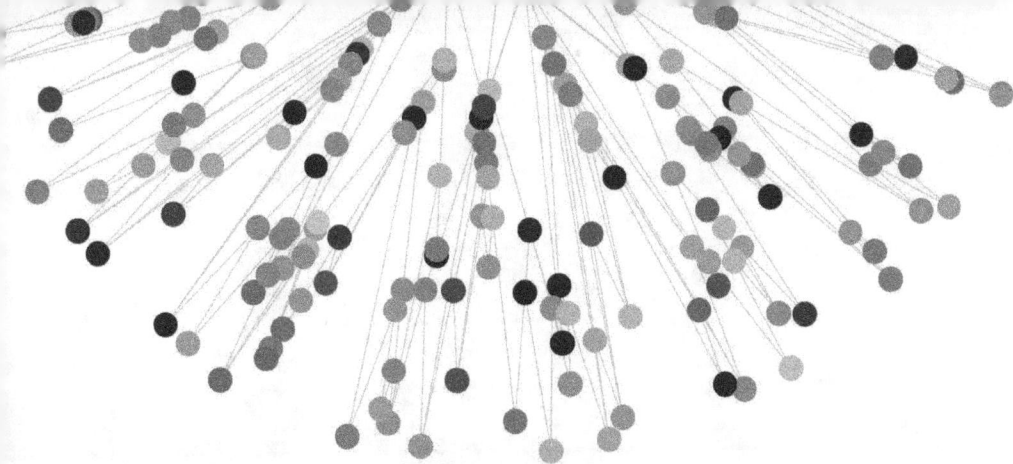

PART 3

CULTIVATING
INTERNAL CULTURE

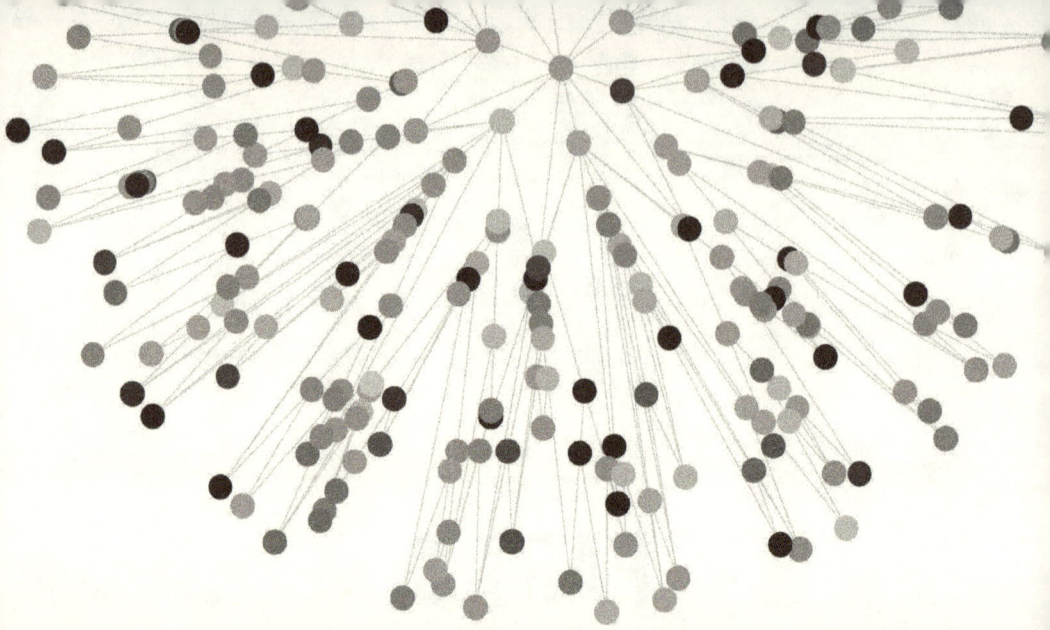

CHAPTER 8

COMPANY CULTURE MATTERS

You can't ignore culture.

—GOLEMAN, BOYATZIS, AND MCKEE[98]

In those early days as interim dean at Protest U, my internet searches yielded little direction in filling the role.

My new boss, the vice president, had directed me to begin my tenure by conducting a faculty review. Reflecting on my experience, I decided it was best to start by listening. With a keen eye on my EQ radar, I began.

Rachel, our faculty's human resources professional, was first. Under the university's centralized model, each HR professional managed a diverse portfolio of faculties and departments.

---

98   Goleman, D., Boyatzis, R. E., & McKee, A. (2013). *Primal leadership: Unleashing the power of emotional intelligence.* Harvard Business Press.

We met in Rachel's office, and as I sat down, she closed the door and asked, "Are you ready for this?" I smiled and shrugged, unsure how to respond and feeling a bit uneasy.

"You have inherited an employee engagement issue," she said.

She supported this claim with significant evidence: numerous staff on stress leave; a catalog of employee grievances, not just with management but also with each other; and a summary of high-profile personnel who had departed for greener grass—but not before berating the institution in scathing exit interviews on their way out the door.

"Sobering" only begins to capture her presentation's effect on me.

I went for a walk after leaving Rachel's office, still processing all I had heard. In the hallways, I noticed office doors closed and sensed uneasiness when I encountered employees, whether in the halls, on the elevator, or in the washrooms.

It made sense: this faculty was depressed—and distressed.

A favorite quote came to mind: "Culture eats strategy for breakfast," attributed to the late Peter Drucker.[99] My faculty had a culture problem.

Blast Zone

This is the group I wrote about in chapter 6, so accustomed to their situation—the gossip about the university possibly closing down the faculty. The faculty needed to find external partners to improve our course offerings, but now it was clear: without also addressing staff morale, our outside engagement efforts might well prove meaningless. My EQ radar sensed my colleagues' dejection, uncertainty, and distrust.

---

99   Drucker, P. F. (2020). *The essential Drucker.* Routledge.

The faculty's problems were an outgrowth of the deterioration of its core business. Enrollments had declined, and in three short years, 130 employees had become 80. As a musician, I rarely count beyond four, but my napkin math put that reduction at almost 40 percent.

I thought about how those who remained must feel, walking by empty offices once occupied by their friends and looking over their shoulders—wondering if they'd be next.

As I built trust, spies brought me information. I learned that those who left on their own had seen the writing on the wall and figured it was better to get out before being laid off, when the rumored detonation of the faculty finally came. They were seen as the lucky ones, my spies reported, whether they were now working at another postsecondary or in another area at Protest U.

Your staff can be your biggest champions—your brand ambassadors—or not. Which will it be?

When employees feel uninspired or disconnected from an organization's mission, vision, and values or feel

MY EMPLOYEES NEEDED TO FEEL THEY WERE FIRST.

like they don't matter, there's a risk to your brand. The existing internal culture was negatively impacting both our brand and our community relationships.

As a fanboy of Sir Richard Branson, the founder of Virgin, I've had the privilege of hearing him speak. This only strengthened my admiration for his corporate philosophy, and I remind myself of his teachings almost daily. In this situation, I remembered his words: "Clients do not come first. Employees come first. If you take care of your employees, they will take care of the clients."[100]

My employees needed to feel they were first.

---

100 Branson, R. (2011). *Losing my virginity*. Random House.

Renovation

If you spoke to my grade school teachers, they'd probably say Little Brad was a good kid who occasionally made bad choices. I remember having to go to the principal's office a few times when I wasn't in trouble, and it was still unnerving; the place had an aura. The couple of times that Little Brad's bad choices found him sitting outside the closed office door, just waiting to be summoned, felt like punishment enough.

As a leader, I remind staff and stakeholders that my office door is always open (but say it with a smile, almost tongue-in-cheek, because I'm seldom at my desk). While I suspect people appreciate the sentiment, in this interim dean role, I felt that I needed to do more to make people feel they could come to me—and that when they did, instead of an empty chair, they'd find a welcoming environment.

I noticed that few came for visits.

One who did, a few times at least, was Louise, our head of registration. Each time, I noted her discomfort, but as our rapport grew—and as I shared my observations with her—she confirmed my suspicions.

Louise confided that just the thought of coming to my office made her heart race, and the visit itself made her tremble. It was a bad anchor that manifested a physiological response. It reminded her of the previous leadership's authoritarian regime, and it reminded me of Little Brad at the principal's office. I thanked her for her candor, and while she wasn't requesting a solution, I promised to think about what we'd discussed.

Doing so, I realized that I, too, felt uncomfortable in my office! It fairly screamed "power," confronting visitors with a large, expensive oak desk. Guests sat in a modest chair on one side of the power desk, while I occupied a large, emperor-style armchair across from them.

How could I make my office feel less hierarchical and more of a psychologically safe space, where people could be open and vulnerable?

After some reflection, I decided to rearrange the furniture—and remove the power desk. My executive assistant was surprised and dismayed.

"That desk was expensive and custom-made for this space," she informed me. I figured someone somewhere would be upset by my furniture decisions, and was certain there'd be paperwork to complete, but held firm: that expansive desk, I knew, was the physical representation of the top-down style that had kept this faculty intimidated rather than invested. I replaced it with a more modest surface that ran parallel to a side wall. The barrier was gone.

Next, a modest circular meeting table, large enough to fit four identical armchairs, was positioned by the large outdoor-facing window. I placed a small plant on the windowsill and a box of Kleenex in the middle of the table. I even replaced the cold corporate artwork with softer, engaging expressions that conveyed warmth and, it turned out, often served as conversation starters.

Grand Opening

I invited Louise back for a meeting.

As she cautiously entered the reimagined space, her eyes widened. With her entrance no longer impeded by the power desk, the open concept invited her farther into the room than she'd ever been. I directed her to the table by the window, and in sync, we pulled our matching chairs away from the table and sat.

Louise's body language and facial expressions signaled ease. We had a great conversation, and upon conclusion, I thanked her for the productive meeting. We even chatted about the artwork on her way out, and her last look included a nod and an assuring smile.

Next, I announced office hours—not only advertising my office's open door but ensuring that I would actually be found in it during the noted times, available for a conversation, no appointment required. The response was positive, and the topics varied.

That two-hour block of time each week produced a potpourri of discussion points. Some employees wanted to muse about the changing learner profile, others to discuss marketing strategies for their programs, and still others to complain about how often their trash can was emptied or the temperature of their office.

If my attention to these things was what people needed to come to work, to feel valued, and to serve our students, community, and other stakeholders, then no subject was too small. In every conversation, I was present, listened, and reframed—my colleagues had to know that I cared about them and their experiences, and visitors left feeling heard.

Listening and learning were my top priorities, but these meetings were also an opportunity to share my values—and I consistently did so. This helped me build rapport not just among the staff who participated, but surprisingly, with those who did not as well.

Employees were sharing their experiences with colleagues, my spies told me. My interactions in the hallways, elevator, and washrooms were also becoming less awkward. More and more office doors were being left open, and even Louise became a regular in my office, even if just poking her head in the doorway to say a quick "Good morning."

Then something interesting happened.

A few months into my new role, a management team member began leaving *her* door open. Then another did. And as those doors opened, conversations took place, and people felt heard.

Trust was building. Our culture was improving. A community was forming.

Still, more work was needed.

Investing in Culture

Building community inside an organization requires providing opportunities for employees to celebrate and nurture personal connections. I have found that the best way to do this is by formalizing interactions and activities through the work of a social committee.

Throughout my administrative career, I have participated in these groups. They typically organize regular potluck lunches, celebrate employee birthdays and milestones, and plan events for major holidays. Yet at Protest U, no such resource existed.

My open-door approach had introduced me to Janice and Kate, who were always friendly and engaged. When I floated the idea of a social committee with them, they were all in.

While they began mapping out ideas, I worked to approve a new budget line—the financial support and promotional support their efforts would require in order to succeed.

I also prioritized being visible and participating in the events Janice and Kate put together to show that these social, team-culture, and internal community-building efforts were valued.

Still, I remained mindful that I was the boss; my presence could detract from the fun for those still wary after years of "walking on eggshells." So I popped into the events and stayed for a short time—mingled, perhaps said a few words, always expressing my sincere gratitude to the social committee. Then, off I went, leaving attendees to fulfill their mission: **connecting**.

The events broadened as the calendar grew to include optional health challenges (like weekly steps competitions), friendly office pools around major sports events, and even after-hours events, from casual postwork refreshments to weekend hiking trips.

The social activities were just the start. There were more investments to make.

The Gift of Time

Having worked in the public sector for most of my life and having many friends who do so as well, I've noticed one glaring difference to the private sector surrounding the performance bonus.

In Western culture, private firms often present lavish holiday staff events and hand out Christmas bonuses—cash rewards to complement an employee's usual salary. The public sector lacks comparable levers to reward staff engagement and company success.

About a year into the interim gig, our student numbers were up. Staff culture had improved significantly. Managers who followed my lead by opening their office doors began bringing forward ideas for advancing our internal culture further still. "They're on the bus!" I thought. I was driving, but they were offering directions, and I listened. After all, they knew the neighborhood.

Many years ago, they explained, a former dean had given staff "the gift of time" during the December holiday season. The office holiday party was scheduled for 11:30 a.m. to 1 p.m., but the calendar invitation set the end time at 4:30 p.m., the school's closing hour. As lunch ended around 1 p.m., staff were encouraged to take the afternoon and do whatever they wished—run errands, get a massage, go home and clean the house, or have a nap—whatever. That slice of paid time was theirs to spend as they saw fit.

I set up a coffee with Cathy, the head of the union, and explained the proposal.

With the employee turmoil at Protest U when my interim tenure began, Cathy and I met monthly to stay connected and discuss various staff situations. Now, a year in, the grievances had stopped, the waters had calmed, and Cathy and I now talked mainly about what we had done the previous weekend. I enjoyed her company.

I walked Cathy through the "gift of time" idea. She liked it. From her perspective, the only risk was to my leadership: I was essentially giving away three to four hours of work time to eighty staff members. Someone somewhere might argue that those 240 to 320 hours of time were productivity lost. **I declared it an investment.**

We gave the gift of time to staff that December and every December thereafter. Employees considered it an investment too—in people's well-being, and a demonstration of management's concern for staff.

Our actions aligned with our words. Our internal community was building, and its inhabitants included staff *and* management.

Culture Matters

Sponsoring social activities and being creative with rewards were well received, and we didn't stop there.

Though the budget was still a work in progress, we reinvested in employee professional development and wellness. It is hard to overstate the importance of nurturing employee growth and happiness. We prioritized both, something I'll detail further in chapter 10.

As outlined in part 2, we invested in our external community through visibility, participation, and sponsorship of events. All these *also* helped build our internal culture. *Forbes* columnist Michael

Timmes writes that employees who see businesses investing in their communities tend to develop a stronger sense of belonging and pride in their organizations.[101]

As previously noted, I've supplemented my lived experience with research. Thought leaders write that strong company culture can improve employee recruitment and retention, especially among younger staff;[102] acknowledge the link between strong corporate culture and improved employee engagement, loyalty, and wellness (through data revealing longer tenures as well as fewer leaves and sick days);[103] and point to culture as a company's single most powerful advantage, linking a strong corporate culture to revenue growth due to increased productivity as employees exceed expectations.[104]

Yet such research and data are not sufficient reasons for embracing this strategy. Building community among your staff must align with *your* values, be heard through *your* genuine voice, and be reflected in *your* vision as a leader.

Back in chapter 1, I talked about emotional intelligence as a vital leadership tool. Daniel Goleman, an EI thought leader, says the key element in group intelligence is not IQ but collective EQ, that social harmony determines a work team's potential.[105] Therefore,

---

101   Timmes, M. (2023). *Why community involvement supports business success*. Forbes. Retrieved from https://www.forbes.com/sites/forbescoachescouncil/2023/07/11/why-community-involvement-supports-business-success/?sh=7dc4666a22fc

102   Alton, L. (2017). Why corporate culture is becoming even more important. *Forbes*. Retrieved from https://www.forbes.com/sites/larryalton/2017/02/17/why-corporate-culture-is-becoming-even-more-important/?sh=3f34df969dac

103   Seppala, E., & Cameron, K. (2015). Proof that positive work cultures are more productive. *Harvard Business Review, 12*(1), 44–50.

104   Laker, B. (2021). Culture is a company's single most powerful advantage. *Forbes*. Retrieved from https://www.forbes.com/sites/benjaminlaker/2021/04/23/culture-is-a-companys-single-most-powerful-advantage-heres-why/?sh=14755642679e

105   Goleman, D.R. (2005). *Emotional intelligence: Why it can matter more than IQ* (10th ed.). New York: Bantam Books.

organizational values of social harmony and internal community must become workplace pillars. In short, social harmony supports effective teamwork, and effective teamwork leads to championships.

Championship Culture

I'm a devoted fan of all sports. Basically, if it keeps score, I follow it.

I was born a Montreal Canadiens fan, but when my family relocated west, I eventually cheered for the Calgary Flames. This, of course, meant that I spent much of my youth being tormented by the Flames' archrivals, Wayne Gretzky's Edmonton Oilers. Throughout the 1980s, the Battle of Alberta, as their showdowns were known, were often one-sided, save a few notable anomalies ('86 and '89).

Gretzky is still known as "the Great One"—a living legend. He shattered almost every offensive record in NHL history on the way to collecting four Stanley Cup rings with Edmonton. When he was famously traded to the Los Angeles Kings in August 1988, many were sure the Cup would follow him south—but that didn't happen. In fact, Edmonton would win another championship (in 1990) without Gretzky.

Michael Jordan's individual stats decorate the record books, but his six championships with the Chicago Bulls keep him in the conversation as perhaps the greatest player ever. MJ said it best: talent wins games, teamwork wins championships.[106]

Perhaps Apple's Steve Jobs was following hockey or basketball when he declared that great things in business are never done by one person, but rather by a team of people.[107] Actually, Jobs's analogy

---

106 Halberstam, D. *Playing for keeps: Michael Jordan and the world he made.* Crown, 2000.

107 Jobs, S. *60 minutes.* (2003, December). CBS Television Network.

referred to the Beatles, perhaps the most revered band in popular music. Still, it made his point: together, teams are greater than the sum of their parts.[108]

I have carried this championship mindset into my leadership roles. At Protest U, we came together and built a community—a team—and success followed.

The reconnection was most obvious first on campus. We heard from colleagues across the university: our cultural shift had rejuvenated staff. As time passed, we saw growing proof of *external* community bonds too. The engaged staff fostered our "Partner of Choice" reputation (chapter 6), and our dance card filled up—we began attracting talent from across the city.

Employer of Choice

All good things must end, and my time at Protest U was no exception. After almost six years, I accepted my next role and would be leaving in six months.

I asked my boss if she still wanted me to chair the hiring committee for a new manager role we'd recently created. I would not be working with the new person, so should I still be involved in selecting them? "You know what's best for the faculty," she said, and reaffirmed her faith in my leadership.

Her words meant a lot to me, and they still do.

The competition's final round included four candidates: one was quasi-internal (from a different department on campus), while the other finalists came from three of the city's other postsecondaries.

"Wow," I thought.

---

108   Jobs, S. *60 minutes*. (2003, December). CBS Television Network.

"We've transformed from a faculty where staff were applying out—moving to other departments on campus or leaving for our competitors—to being a destination."

We'd fulfilled my aspirations, becoming not just a partner of choice, but an employer of choice as well.

I had consistently reinforced a competitive total compensation package as our minimum objective for new hires. I believed that by exceeding employment standards and employee expectations, the responses to our job postings would prove our success. Or not.

The interviews with our final four were enlightening. The candidates shared that they were attracted to Protest U by stories of our corporate culture and community engagement: they wanted to join. *We* had become the greener grass.

WE'D FULFILLED MY ASPIRATIONS, BECOMING NOT JUST A PARTNER OF CHOICE, BUT AN EMPLOYER OF CHOICE AS WELL.

The university placed an interim dean in my vacant role and, several months later, started a search to fill it permanently. A search firm was hired, and community conversation ensued.

Through the grapevine, I heard that my past colleagues were vocal about the value of their corporate culture, and the internal community we had built together. They wanted assurances that the university's senior administration and the search firm's consultants would look for a new leader with similar values.

We'd righted the financial ship too—from annual six-figure deficits to annual seven-figure surpluses.

We felt like champions.

Closing Thoughts

A healthy, caring culture radiates outward. People-centric cultures impact and drive results. Make values, empathy, and humanity central. Invest in people. Nurture connections—and *joy*. When community is built both outside *and* inside, engagement follows.

Internal community building requires broad employee buy-in. As a leader, you must champion this value. Authors Senge, Hamilton, and Kania discuss a "systems leader"—someone who promotes collective leadership and brings together those who are divided.[109] An ability to unite and onboard a divided staff—and to point them toward the achievement of a shared, *cocreated* vision—are crucial tools.

A HEALTHY, CARING CULTURE RADIATES OUTWARD.

Bob Chapman, CEO and author of *Everybody Matters: The Extraordinary Power of Caring for Your People Like Family*, writes about the process of building community within a business. He quotes his friend, Lt. Gen. George Flynn, USMC (ret.): culture equals values plus behavior.[110]

Values can be inscribed on company literature and assets, but *behavior* must be modeled by you, the leader. Because, as Daniel Goleman reminds us, employees are always watching you,[111] a truth we'll explore fully in our next chapter.

109 Senge, P., Hamilton, H., & Kania, J. (2015). The dawn of system leadership. *Stanford Social Innovation Review, 13*(1), 27–33.

110 Chapman, B., Sisodia, R., & Sisodia, R. (2015). *Everybody matters: The extraordinary power of caring for your people like family.* Portfolio.

111 Goleman, D., Boyatzis, R. E., & McKee, A. (2013). *Primal leadership: Unleashing the power of emotional intelligence.* Harvard Business Press.

Key Takeaways

This chapter explored building community *inside* your company as the key to engaging your *external* community.

- Culture impacts brand and engagement.

- People-centric, "championship" cultures drive results.

- Inside bonds strengthen outside ties.

For Reflection

Data from our human resources folks provided me a baseline for my situation at Protest U. Whether you have such data or not, enlisting the help of your staff will fast-track an accurate assessment of your organization's current culture.

With that assessment in hand, identify three areas of focus for building a healthier, more caring workplace community.

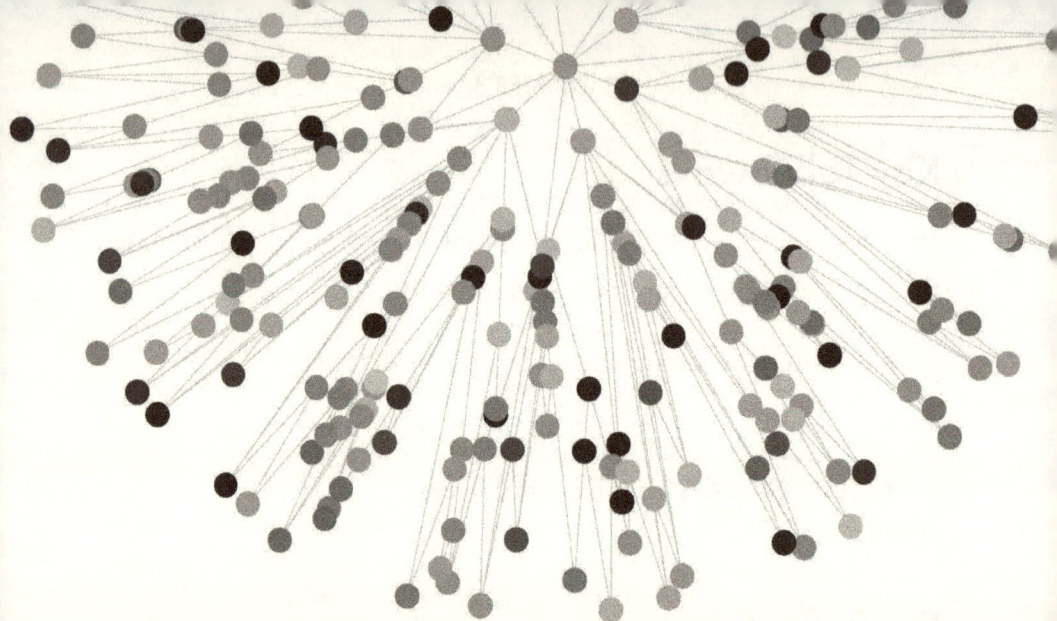

CHAPTER 9

LEAD BY EXAMPLE

A leader is one who knows the way, goes the way, and shows the way.

—JOHN MAXWELL[112]

A woman approached me when I was at a community college event. "Are you *Brad from the college*?" she asked. I smiled and confirmed her suspicion, and she said her community group had started holding its board meetings on campus.

"I'd never been inside the college before. I went to the information desk, and the young lady was so friendly," she enthused, paying one of our staff a nice compliment. "She explained the way, but I think she sensed my confusion. So she just walked me there herself instead!"

I noticed the smile on her face. She felt welcome at the college, and I thanked her for telling me so. I thought of Tzu's *Art of War* and

---

112   Maxwell, J. C. (2007). *The 21 irrefutable laws of leadership: Follow them and people will follow you.* HarperCollins Leadership.

his reference to spies.[113] Thanks to my visibility in the community, I received valuable intel often.

Daniel Goleman has said that a team's success is more influenced by its collective EQ than its communal IQ.[114] So how do we build social harmony in our workplaces? The previous chapter offered some solutions. Here, we'll focus on another facet of the construction process: **modeling social harmony yourself**.

When a particularly distinguished group visited campus, I made sure to greet them at our main entrance as they arrived. Sometimes I'd walk them to the room myself, where we'd continue to chat. I practiced this throughout my tenure, and it always produced the sense that by modeling how to represent the college, I might inspire staff to follow my lead.

Earlier in my career, however, I was not always so pleased with my actions.

Three years into my role as a dean, the global COVID-19 pandemic hit, and remote work became the norm. We had achieved great things as a faculty, and surprisingly, staff culture actually improved during the lockdown, thanks to communication, communication, communication (more in chapter 11).

Yet in the earliest weeks of the pandemic, I contradicted my values and failed to model the behaviors I wanted our internal community to adopt.

---

113   Tzu, S. (1994). *The art of war*. Basic Books.

114   Goleman, D. R. (2005). *Emotional intelligence: Why it can matter more than IQ* (10th ed.). New York: Bantam Books.

Groundhog Day

Bill Murray's *Groundhog Day* is a cult classic. If you disagree, it's one more reason we can't be friends.

In the movie, Murray wakes up each morning to find the day's events are an exact rerun of the past twenty-four hours.[115] Though it was released in 1993, I found myself thinking about the movie more than twenty-five years later. It was the spring of 2020, and the world had just closed.

Leading during that time was wild. I remember working longer days than I ever had and feeling like, just when we'd found a path forward, health restrictions changed again, and it was back to the drawing board. It was one of the most challenging times of my leadership journey.

I remember feeling tired, always. Leaders are always working, but working from home meant being *at work all the time.* The boundary between my personal and professional lives vanished, at a moment when thinking about oneself was rightly secondary.

In short, our leadership team was attempting to guide an organization through something no organization had navigated before.

At Protest U, we closed the campus and instructed faculty, students, and staff to work remotely until further notice, but it soon became clear that certain business functions required employees to be on-site. We had no option but to declare some workers essential and order them back to campus.

The recalled workers' unhappiness—and defiance—were palpable. The productive and harmonious environment we had worked so hard to build was shattered, the changes affecting not only their work but

---

115   Ramis, H. (1993). *Groundhog Day.* Columbia Pictures.

also their morale. They were afraid of becoming sick and understandably angry about being "forced" back to campus.

We took every safety precaution we knew of, but much was still unknown. This, coupled with considerable misinformation about the virus, created fear. Staff bitterness grew toward senior administration. Resentment toward employees still working from home also took hold.

We've all heard it: "The captain goes down with the ship." So, modeling my support for essential staff, I offered to work on campus too. I do not believe in asking employees to do something I won't do myself.

However, the health people trumped me—*only* essential people would be permitted on campus; fewer people interacting with each other was best for everyone's health. In these earliest days, as the global death toll mounted, fear was pervasive.

Since I wasn't allowed to work on campus, I regularly dropped by with coffee and muffins, a small expression of my gratitude. But my EQ radar sensed the staff were cool to these efforts.

It wasn't that their return to work had happened, my spies revealed. What bothered staff was *how* it all went down: our essential workers felt they'd been ordered back to campus without an explanation or rationale.

Naturally, I justified my actions to myself. At the time, I felt like we were at war—battling a virus that people didn't understand, with life-or-death implications. There was no time for discussion. "This is war—follow my orders," I thought.

I was wrong.

In an environment of fear, I *added* to the uncertainty. By choosing not to show empathy and seek understanding, I wasn't walking the talk by modeling my expectations. I hadn't put myself in the shoes of the staff who were ordered back to campus.

My reflection, and the realization it prompted, was sobering. I called an online staff meeting for all who had been ordered back to work.

After reminding everyone of the foundation we'd built—our few years as colleagues and of all we had built together—I expressed my sincere desire for renewed dialogue and let them know that they were in a safe place to provide it.

It worked. And they let me have it.

Months of fear and frustration poured out. My EQ radar lit up. Their emotions peaked. The meeting felt like an erupting volcano. How could I keep the discussion productive and the meeting from getting away from me?

Slow Motion

On January 11, 1987, the Denver Broncos played the Cleveland Browns in the conference finals. The winner would earn a trip to the National Football League's Super Bowl.

To be clear, I didn't care who won. As a Chicago Bears fan, I hoped for an incredible scenario in which both teams lost. But what I and millions of others who saw the game still remember about that day is Denver quarterback John Elway.

With five minutes to go, Elway had the mammoth task of leading his team the entire length of the field before eighty thousand unfriendly Cleveland fans who were not shy about voicing their disapproval of every successful Denver play. Systematically, he authored a fifteen-play, 98-yard scoring drive that tied the game with thirty-nine seconds left. The Broncos added a field goal in overtime, sealing the win and punching their Super Bowl ticket.

That sequence of plays is cemented in NFL history as "the Drive." It also cemented Elway's reputation as a "clutch" player and leader, able to deliver results in a hostile, high-stakes environment. Similar examples exist throughout history from other sports.

I thought again of Wayne Gretzky. I still had scars from his heartbreaking performances during the '80s' Battles of Alberta, yet he also fascinated me. How was he so great? Like other elite athletes, he talked about being able to *slow the game down*, especially in high-stakes moments.[116]

My mind even wandered toward Peter Parker, a.k.a. Spider-Man.[117]

Director Sam Raimi's 2002 reboot of the franchise offered moviegoers a view of the world through the superhero's eyes. Spider-Man's incredible reaction time stemmed, in part, from internal perception—*his* reality moved slower. In critical moments, Parker's Spidey Sense kicked in, enabling him to view the world in slow motion and react to threats.[118]

They all flashed through my mind in this staff meeting—Elway, Gretzky, and Parker. I spent most of my high school football career on the bench. I never skated very well. And I'd never been bitten by a radioactive spider.

But I *had* read my Gallwey and my Goleman!

I engaged in active listening and empathy: others were emotionally heightened; some spoke abruptly and quickly. So I took every opportunity to slow the pace of the meeting by creating space after each person spoke.

I ensured my responses were spoken *andante*—at a walking pace. I wanted to ensure the staff that they were truly being heard and that

---

116   Gretzky, W., & Reilly, R. (1990). *Gretzky, an autobiography*. Harper & Collins.

117   Lee, S. (1962). *Spider-Man*. Marvel Comics.

118   Raimi, S. (2002). *Spider-Man*. Columbia Pictures.

I was relating to their perspectives. I showed no defensiveness in my facial expressions and kept my body language "open," listened to understand, and tried to imagine how each staff member must have felt over these difficult months.

I had not been the leader they needed and, more importantly, deserved. I had to start now.

I TOLD THEM THAT IF I COULD GO BACK IN TIME, I WOULD HAVE DONE THINGS DIFFERENTLY.

The emotions lowered; the conversation slowed. It was time for me to speak. My voice was soft. I spoke slower than usual, and my tone conveyed reflection and remorse.

I admitted my mistakes, acknowledged my poor communication, and apologized. I showed vulnerability, admitting that my words and actions had been out of alignment with our core values. I had not been leading with consistency at the precise moment that authentic leadership was most critically needed.

I told them that if I could go back in time, I would have done things differently.

And then, I got specific.

I told them what I *would* have said—and what I *should* have said—months ago, before they ever returned to campus. I detailed the *why* around their return and the critical role they played in the success of our institution and our students. And I finished by sharing with them how much our entire school community valued what they do.

The conversation organically shifted to ideas about how to move forward. Staff talked about their time back on campus, and we discussed steps I could take toward improving their daily experience. We formed an action plan and a communication plan. The meeting ended with universal senses of relief and hope.

From that day forward, I met virtually with essential staff each week, independent of our weekly all-faculty meetings, where I consistently acknowledged the on-campus staff and their important work. Essential staff joined my management team as the only two groups with which I had regularly scheduled, private sessions.

Working with the essential staff's direct supervisors, we examined their duties in depth, identifying some tasks that could be done remotely. This allowed essential staff to begin hybrid work, splitting their time between campus and home.

Through it all, we strengthened an already strong community. Communication and celebration were key aspects of the process, which we'll examine in greater detail in chapter 11.

First Impressions

I still remember the first time I saw Darth Vader. It was the late '70s, and a wide-eyed Little Brad clutched his popcorn bag, absorbed by the Dark Lord's ominous presence in the dim movie theater.

It was the opening scene of *Episode IV*. The *Star Wars* villain emerged through a cloud of smoke—the remnants of laser fire from moments before.[119] He coldly glanced at the bodies on the ground, stepping over them as he walked the ship's corridor, the scene of the recent battle. His aura was threatening, and it was just the start.

What made Darth Vader so terrifying was his disregard for everyone except his boss, the emperor.

Sure, the rebels were the enemy, but his interactions with his coworkers revealed his values and voice. The movie exposed a leader who leveraged terror: an ominous voice, constant threats to his staff, and instant death upon failure. Director George Lucas was sure to capture the Imperial employees' faces, and the mutual glances that reinforced their distress.

---

119   Lucas, G. (1977). *Star wars episode IV: A new hope*. 20th Century.

Vader's leadership behaviors also affected how his colleagues treated others—shooting first, never asking questions or seeking to understand, name-calling, and showing an overall lack of compassion.

It was quite a first impression.

We've all heard the axiom, "You never get a second chance to make a first impression." It's been attributed to a variety of people, and some have done scholarly research around the impact of first impressions.[120] But whoever coined that platitude, it bubbles up for me when I meet someone for the first time.

Remember the Haunted Hall gig? I had arrived early on day one and wandered around, really soaking in the experience, but I had no keys!

When staff arrived shortly before 8:00 a.m., the receptionist called the custodian to open my office door. She kindly waited with me for him to arrive. A few other staff members noticed us and walked over to introduce themselves. It was my first interaction with the staff, and the chatter back and forth was easy.

The custodian arrived and opened the door, revealing that the one-time office was now a storage space! Cardboard boxes were stacked everywhere—on the floor, the desk, and the meeting table. The assembled staff were alarmed and embarrassed and immediately became nervous.

The custodian broke the tension. He quickly surmised that the office had become a temporary storage space in the absence of the previous department head, who had departed months before. My EQ radar lit up; everyone seemed to be waiting for my reaction.

---

120 Harris, M. J., & Garris, C. P. (2008). You never get a second chance to make a first impression: Behavioral consequences of first impressions.

I smiled, let out a soft chuckle, and sensed that my amusement disarmed them. Then I spoke: "All these boxes make it look just like my apartment. I feel at home already!"

Now everyone chuckled, and my first day had begun.

I could have shown frustration: *Why wasn't my office ready?* But what message would that have sent?

Instead, I modeled the behaviors I hoped to see in others, consciously demonstrating the desired conduct. It didn't matter why the office wasn't ready, and I didn't care whose fault it was. My sole focus was on *how to resolve it.*

A colleague showed me to the staff room (where the coffee was—critically important!), and by the time we had strolled back, the custodian had been joined by a few maintenance staff. Decisions about where the boxes would go were being made.

> INSTEAD, I MODELED THE BEHAVIORS I HOPED TO SEE IN OTHERS, CONSCIOUSLY DEMONSTRATING THE DESIRED CONDUCT.

I genuinely thanked everyone for their efforts and expressed my appreciation for the warm welcome exemplified by their help.

Staff will talk about you when you are not around; that's a given. But your actions and reactions are what shape that chatter. I like to think that by demonstrating that I lived my values and displaying them in action, that first day set a positive tone.

Prairie Winters

It was just before 5:00 a.m., and my phone was ringing. It was the building manager of our performing arts center with what I suspected was bad news.

Winters on the Canadian prairies are always cold, but we were having an especially cold stretch. You knew it was bad when even longtime locals complained, and only the long-term forecast offered the hope of relief.

The building manager's animated voice confirmed my suspicion: frigid arctic temperatures had caused a sprinkler line to burst near the concert hall's roof. Water was everywhere, and the $100 million state-of-the-art facility was only a few years old.

The campus response was swift, and external support was strong too. After briefing me thoroughly and sharing photos, the facilities manager encouraged me to stay home (translation: out of the way) and promised regular updates.

I advised senior leadership that the experts were at work on the issue. In fact, the quick work of staff reduced what could have been an eight-figure mess to "only" a seven-figure mess.

We agreed on a comms plan, including mass emails and social media posts, but many of our faculty were also performing artists who rarely checked their university email accounts. What would they—and other faculty, students, and staff—make of the emergency vehicles surrounding the building upon their arrival? What would they hear as they were turned away, likely by a stranger?

With the main *Star Wars* theme trumpeting in my head, I dressed quickly and dashed out the door. The early hour meant city traffic would be no obstacle, and I arrived before sunrise. Lights from emergency vehicles illuminated the still-dark sky as I neared campus.

I worked to calm my racing thoughts. I talked my way past security and met with our facilities group to assess the damage. It was bad. But creating a plan to fix the damage was a plan for another day. In that moment, my thoughts centered on our people.

I went back outside just as the first arrivals pulled into the parking lot. I met cars carrying students, faculty, and staff and provided a quick summary at each driver's open window. After an awkward start, I was soon reciting my key messages in about twenty seconds.

As time passed, it became (frost)bitingly clear that I was under-dressed—I had rushed out my front door unprepared for the brutal cold. But a group effort kicked in: staff ran to the campus store and returned with layers for me, including branded hats, gloves, and appropriate winter wear.

As they dressed me, I took on a mascotlike appearance. The best moment was covering the motley collection of winter wear with the school's hockey jersey, which was fitting in more ways than one.

More cars arrived, and I now struggled to keep up with the volume. Amazingly, other faculty and staff joined me—bundled up, of course—in giving each arriving teammate the key messages. Soon, senior admin colleagues from other faculties and departments joined the effort.

The response of our internal community to this situation was wonderful. It offered further validation for leading by example.

Despite our emails and social media posts when the news broke, only afterward did I hear about the power of my presence, wandering the frigid parking lot and speaking to stakeholders in person. Silently, my actions called others to action. The building was eventually repaired and reopened, and my lasting memory of that difficult day is its collegiality, collaboration, and community building.

Reflecting with Others

Years later, I still think about the first months of the pandemic. Jeffrey Morales, business development manager at Anheuser-Busch, talks about the need to communicate in a respectful manner—don't just tell your team members what you want, but explain to them *why*.[121]

Upon reflection, I should've shown more empathy to the staff that I sent back to campus to work. My communication to the essential workers should've been better.

The decision was correct—its rollout, not so much. In hindsight, I would've handled the situation differently, being more empathetic to essential staff's respective and collective emotions and concerns.

My time machine was in the shop, though, so it was incumbent upon *me* to initiate a process that might make this bad situation better, including asking their forgiveness.

> TO ANY LEADER, I WOULD SAY: IT STARTS, CONTINUES, AND FINISHES WITH *YOU.*

As part of my own best practice, I have studied literature and talked with other influential leaders about how, by modeling desired behaviors, their team culture improved and how they consciously modeled values *through* their behaviors. I wanted to know how they "walked the talk."

One leader reminded me that staff hang on your every word; thus, we must always be aware of our voice and actions.

Trey Taylor writes that the world hungers for authenticity, that we all want something real in our lives—somewhere safe to place our trust, someone we can believe in.[122]

Work consumes so much of our time. Our employees deserve a culture they can thrive in. Build a community your employees feel safe in. As Simon Sinek says, be the leader you wish you had.[123]

121 Trembicki, M. (2024). *The importance of communication.* Amplify. Retrieved from https://www.amprg.com/the-importance-of-communication

122 Taylor, T. (2002). *CEO excellence.* Advisors Board.

123 Sinek, S. (2014). *Leaders eat last: Why some teams pull together and others don't.* Penguin.

To any leader, I would say: it starts, continues, and finishes with *you*.

Upon reflection, I have discovered that *my* actions are like a pebble dropped in a still pond—those ripples affect my team, which affects our clients, which affects our business, and all of it directly impacts our overall success or failure. So work on *you* first, then lead by design—by setting an example, by teaching and mentoring, and by investing in your people.

Closing Thoughts

Aspirations for an organization must begin with culture: the professional environment that *is* the workplace. A company's success relies on the fulsome contributions of an engaged and committed faculty and staff. This ethos begins with leadership.

Administration must be transparent, accountable, accessible, communicative, and open-minded—reflecting on and considering differing perspectives. The professional culture must be one of teamwork, where trust, collaboration, empathy, and forgiveness are valued.

I have aspired to and cultivated an "employer of choice" environment. Statistical analysis of our efforts bears this out, revealing low employee turnover, minimal sick and leave time, significant applications to new internal job postings, and documented reports of elevated employee engagement and declared satisfaction.

I have learned that being successful starts with me. I need to believe in, and live, what I am selling.

But what *am* I selling? Ultimately, I'm selling *me*—myself, as a model. I'm selling my interpersonal skills. I'm selling my behaviors. I'm selling my values, my reactions, and my rapport. I'm selling my approaches to building relationships, forming new partnerships, addressing conflict, finding resolution, and investing in employees.

Leaders' actions speak louder than their words. Values must be lived. As a leader, *you* set the tone. Walk your talk. Model desired behaviors. Live your values visibly. And not performatively, but sincerely. Admit mistakes. Listen and empathize. Modeling values builds trust. Model your expectations, and your team will follow.

Key Takeaways

In this chapter, we explored the importance of modeling desired behaviors and values as a leader. Your team is watching, so remember:

- Leaders' actions speak louder than their words.
- Modeling your values builds trust.
- Consistency enables cultural change.

For Reflection

Pick a key value and consciously model it through your daily behaviors and interactions for the next week. Notice how doing so feels and how colleagues seem to perceive it. When satisfied, add another value to your repertoire. Throughout your tenure, repeat, repeat, repeat.

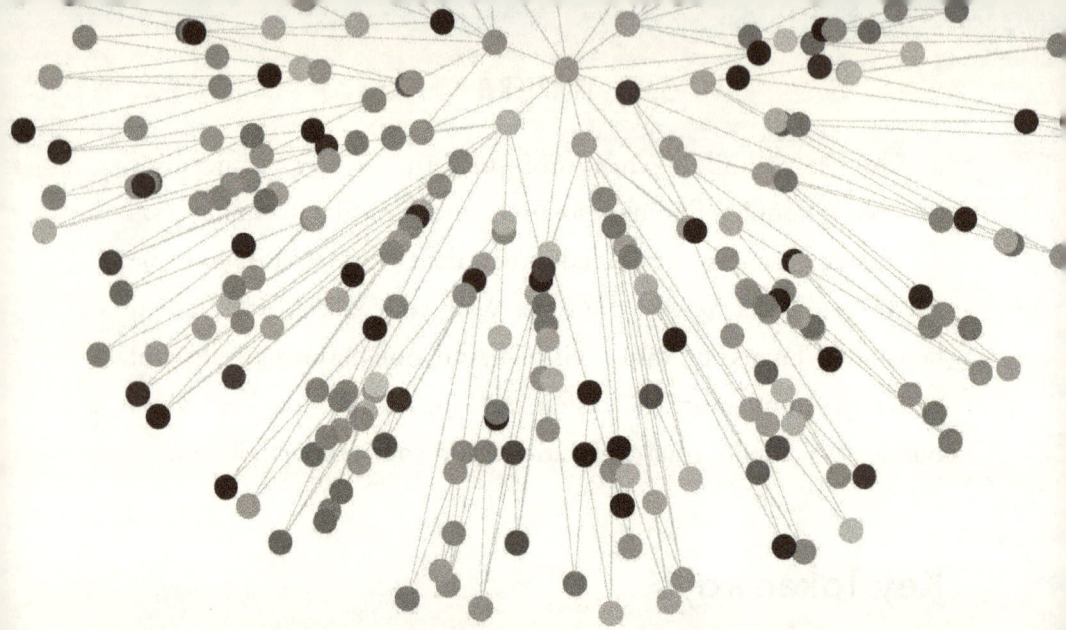

CHAPTER 10

VALUES-BASED HIRING

Acquiring the right talent is the most important key to growth. Hiring was—and still is—the most important thing we do.

—MARC BENIOFF[124]

The light was green. We were ready to offer the job to our first-choice candidate. The hiring committee beamed with satisfaction and radiated energy—we felt assured of our choice.

We had just spent four months searching for our newest executive colleague, and through the process, we'd grown close—a community.

I was relieved for a few reasons: (1) we had found a great person, (2) I felt connected to my colleagues on the committee, and (3) our newly overhauled recruitment process had worked.

---

124 Benioff, M., & Adler, C. (2009). *Behind the cloud: The untold story of how Salesforce. com went from idea to billion-dollar company and revolutionized an industry.* John Wiley & Sons.

I had been with the organization just six months when the time came to search for my right-hand person. My tenure was limited, but some practices within our HR department had prompted questions for me, particularly around staffing.

Our hiring practices were so conventional that they were dated. They felt clinical and stale, as if taken from an early edition of an HR textbook.

Studying other models, I noticed that even "human resources" was becoming a dated term. Things like "people and culture" or "talent acquisition" permeated HR staff titles elsewhere, and it was more than just window dressing; it was about mindset and strategy. Other ideas percolated for me from lived experience at other organizations, and through my love of sports.

Scouting Report

You will see various things when you look on a job board or employment website, but you won't see this:

Professional hockey team looking for an annual fifty-goal scorer.

Applicants should include a cover letter and résumé.

Sports teams take a different approach to finding and acquiring talent, and their approach is surprisingly instructive.

Professional and amateur teams have scouting departments: dedicated people who are *constantly* looking for talent, not just when there's an open roster spot. Identifying and courting talent must always be top of mind—you must always be looking.

Bob McKenzie, one of The Sports Network's[125] premier hockey analysts, consistently updates his talent roster. It is quantified and qualified, ranks the best prospects, and explains why. While pro-

---

125   The Sports Network. Toronto. Retrieved from https://www.tsn.ca/

fessional teams have their own personnel conducting similar work, McKenzie is usually spot-on with his analyses and predictions, which often match actual outcomes.

Attention is given to established players too. The Sports Network's *Trade Bait* show regularly ranks (and reranks) top players, focusing on those possibly available for acquisition.

And though statistics matter, it's not always the top goal scorers who go first in the draft or rank high on the trade list. Evaluators are sure to assess and consider a player's character—the leadership chops they bring to the ice and the locker room.

My point? Competencies matter, but the character and values of players matter too.

Hockey is a big part of my Canadian upbringing, but North America's three other top sports—baseball, basketball, and football— have similar processes, and the point is the same: these organizations don't sit back and wait for what they will eventually need. They actively look for it, 24/7/365.

> COMPETENCIES MATTER, BUT THE CHARACTER AND VALUES OF PLAYERS MATTER TOO.

That's understandable: these players can markedly impact organizations, in both the win column and their team's profit-and-loss statement. Why, I wondered, don't *we* approach talent the same way?

Renovation Required

A fellow senior leader once told me, "Every vacancy is an opportunity." She was right, but in my first year at Grasslands College, there were other fires to extinguish.

Still, I realized that beyond its conventionality of process, our approach to recruiting was mechanical. Duties were defined, aptitudes identified, and the college's mandate and history explained. Our small, siloed hiring committees prioritized *skills*.

My thinking held that while competencies are important, they could also be taught, especially if an organization invests in its people. I believed we needed to look at candidates more deeply, through a *values* lens, and seek perspectives from staff up and down the organizational ladder.

My concerns were validated by the negative consequences of hiring solely for competencies—specifically, disjointed teams. I ignored my intuition and convinced myself I was dealing with higher-level demands—those other fires I mentioned. And the organization paid the price.

Remember VP Vince from chapters 2 and 4? He's back.

I allowed Vince and our HR lead to conduct the search for a vacant manager position in isolation. This was our typical hiring committee: the candidate's would-be supervisor and HR. It seemed logical on the surface, but the process did little to foster inclusion and community in our most important decisions: who works for us and who doesn't.

Gavin was hired quickly and without broader consultation. On paper, he had the experience and checked most of the competency boxes. His hiring was a failure.

Just weeks into his tenure, spies overwhelmed me with reports.

Across my first year, I'd used my voice to cultivate the values of regional cooperation, building a unified campus community—painting a one-college vision rather than six independent campuses, three geographic regions, or north versus south. We wanted our campuses to "stop looking over each other's fences" (i.e., worrying about which campus had what resources and why [usually] theirs did not). We needed instead to foster collaboration and share our often-limited resources.

Gavin pointed the ship in the opposite direction, cultivating an "us versus them" mindset and, worse, seeking out those in the organization who shared his attitude. As they empowered each other and fed their shared sentiments, things went bad—quickly.

"Divisive" only begins to capture the fallout.

Gavin left the organization after just a few months, but undoing the damage took years. It was a wake-up call: *this* was the fire I needed to fight. Without shared values, alignment is impossible.

We needed to start hiring for *values* fit.

The Business of People

As you well know by now, values have been foundational to my daily practice and decision-making as a leader. They are everything. We needed to bring this same view to our hiring practices.

The HR department had some capabilities: policies, procedures, contract management, and employment regulations were handled competently—we had a foundation. But what about treating our workforce as our greatest resource?

If we were selling running shoes, we'd examine the materials that comprise the product: the quality of the sole, the fabric that covers the foot, the laces. We'd judge the overall quality of the shoe by how they all came together.

WE WERE HIRING PEOPLE TO DEVELOP PEOPLE.

But we weren't selling running shoes—we were hiring people to develop people.

Then, we hired more people to support those first two groups of people. It was clear to anyone willing to look: we were in the *people* business.

So we needed to understand what our prospects were made of—what they valued. Did their values align with our organization's? In chapter 1, I said that your values are your values—there's no right or wrong. However, the foundation for building community *is* the values of its parts, and if a prospective employee's values do not align, they cannot join the team.

Screening for Culture

Competencies still mattered, of course, but we started evolving our hiring practices, carefully screening candidates for cultural add, as one example, and exploring their alignment with our values, voice, and vision. The search for our new executive teammate felt like the right time to embrace that new approach.

We started by writing and posting a job ad that went beyond competencies, to the kind of person we were looking for—their essential character and qualities.

Next, I made myself available for one-on-one phone calls with each prospective candidate, including those just thinking about applying. I kept it casual—an opportunity to hear their voice as they asked questions, and for them to hear mine as I answered.

Yes, it was time consuming. Yet these many conversations not only strengthened my values and vision but also my ability to *articulate* both. And I'd wager they were a net time-saver for the organization, as they tended to screen as many potential applicants out as were screened in. I'd sometimes end a call and think, "I hope that person officially applies; I'd like to learn more about them." Other times, it was, "Gosh, that was awkward."

There's simply too much at stake in these hires not to lean into all the intel and signals available.

I also shoulder-tapped people I knew or knew of, and about whom I wanted to learn more. Going in, I ensured they understood that the process would be fair and transparent; I was only offering them the opportunity to explore, to engage in the process to see if there was a mutual fit.

In yet another change, we diversified our hiring committees, moving from a single supervisor and HR lead to committee members equal to, above, and below the vacant position. That diversity brought rich perspectives, and our internal conversations strengthened our commitment to each other and to our organizational values.

As the process neared completion—the championship—the hiring committee took each finalist out for a meal, and conversation, which often *further* exposed value alignment and organizational fit.

It was nothing short of a completely renovated hiring process, but it was not the end of our work. A crucial last step remained.

Welcome to the Show

We hired Jim to be our next chief financial officer. He was experienced and had lots of letters after his name, and our values aligned.

But as well as our reimagined hiring process had worked, ensuring Jim's smooth integration to our culture was the final step, one as critical to employee (and organizational) success as the hiring process itself.

On Jim's first day, I met him at the building's entrance. We started by showing Jim around and introducing him to his new teammates.

We spent the day walking around campus, engaging in quick, casual hallway introductions, stopping for coffee at the campus's popular café, popping into a few of the departments and service areas we interacted with most, and visiting the executive offices for introductions to some of the institution's senior-most leaders.

This day of what's known in the HR world as onboarding added to the foundation we had laid during the recruitment and hiring process.

It was also a chance for me to demonstrate to Jim—and, importantly, to reinforce for my team—my desired behaviors and to live my values (as we discussed in the previous chapter). Opportunities to muse about philosophical topics important to me arose organically, and I took them when they did, usually sharing a favorite anecdote to illustrate, but always ensuring the new employee there'd be no test before I'd leave him or her to their work.

Often, I'd share Warren Buffett's quote: "The greatest investment you can make is in yourself."[126] It was a great way to discuss the employee's career, to encourage them to continue learning, and to signal my support for such growth. While I hoped they would have a long career at our organization, my broader priority was their professional success and fulfillment. If that meant supporting their transition to another role down the road, here or elsewhere, so be it. Others had done the same for me.

Remember Mentor Mike, who had advised me about "living in the weeds," and shared the "watering hole" analogy with me? Well, at one time, Mike was my boss.

One day, he sent me an email with a job ad for the role at Faraway U. I was surprised. We organized a coffee meeting.

After a few sips of deliciousness and some small talk, the conversation shifted to the topic at hand. I teased Mike a little: "Are you trying to get rid of me?" He chuckled. "Brad, there's nothing here for you. This is an opportunity for you to grow, and to *grow*, you need to *go*."

Mike was a five-star reference for me; the rest is history.

---

126 Hagstrom, R. G. (2024). *The Warren Buffett way*. John Wiley & Sons.

I always share that story with staff so they'll know how much I appreciate Mike. He did what was best for *me*, not what was best for the organization. **His selflessness changed my life.**

Throughout my leadership journey, I have been questioned about the logic behind investing in staff development. "They'll just leave anyhow," people will say, or my favorite: "You're training them for someone else."

Of course, there's always a risk that folks will take the education and experience you've provided them and depart. There's always a next chapter; the Beatles broke up and went on to successful solo careers, Tom Brady left the New England Patriots and won a Super Bowl in Tampa Bay the very next year, and that employee you have mentored and invested in might well resign for another opportunity tomorrow.

But by reflecting on some favorite leadership readings, I can see the bigger picture.

I've mentioned my admiration for Virgin's Sir Richard Branson. I hold to his idea to train people well enough so they can leave, yet treat them well enough so they don't want to.[127] Platitudinal? Perhaps. But also, in my experience, *absolutely true.*

Peter Baeklund, meanwhile, tells the story of his CFO asking, "What if we invest in developing our people and they leave us?" Mr. Baeklund turned the question around: "What if we don't invest in them and they stay?"[128]

Part of treating people right is supporting them throughout *all* aspects of their careers, including their transition out of your organization.

---

127 Branson, R. (2014). *The Virgin way: Everything I know about leadership.* Penguin.

128 Bertuzzi, T. (2016). *The sales development playbook: Build repeatable pipeline and accelerate growth with inside sales.* Moore-Lake.

I remember being presented with an excellent professional opportunity. After consulting with family and a few trusted friends, I accepted the new role. I gave my boss several months' notice to help with the transition. Honestly, it became super awkward. The details are long lost to my memory, but I remember how I felt. My relief at finally walking out the door for the last time was all-encompassing; things had become that uncomfortable.

It didn't have to be that way, and the experience is why I now strive to ensure it never is, for those whose paths diverge from ours.

I give new employees my time—in walkabouts, coffees, or meetings. I don't use our meetings to tell or teach about every topic that comes to mind. Instead, I use onboarding sessions to continue building the foundation of a trusting, values-based relationship. Sure, new hires also meet with IT and get set up

NEW HIRES ARE NOT JUST JOINING A COMPANY; THEY ARE BECOMING A MEMBER OF OUR COMMUNITY.

with their corporate machinery, and HR guides them through the necessary policies and forms.

But onboarding, for me, is about *values*. New hires are not just joining a company; they are becoming a member of our community.

I'm with the Band

As a professional guitarist-for-hire, I've played a lot of weddings and wedding receptions. Hundreds. That's a lot of prayers, vows, declarations, poems, and toasts, but there was one speech I'll never forget. An uncle toasted the bride and groom with this story:

I was a car-less young man and managed to arrange a ride into the city with my neighbors Tex and Edna. It was a hot summer day. Tex was driving, his elbow resting on the ledge of his opened window. Edna was on the other side of the cab, leaning somewhat out her opened window. I was sitting in the truck's back seat, just enjoying whatever breeze I could.

A sporty red short-box truck roared past. As it pulled away, we looked through the back window and noticed what looked like the truck's two-headed driver. His passenger had cozied right up, thigh to thigh.

Edna sighed and, half shouting above the airstream enveloping the car, said: "Aw, Tex, look at that! Remember when that was us, no matter how hot it was outside?"

In a total deadpan, Tex called back: "I've never moved."

The audience chuckled as the uncle encouraged the young couple to keep the spark of young romance burning brightly.

How does this story apply to our employees? It speaks to the importance of keeping that honeymoon mindset—of working to appreciate and engage your staff as fully as you did when recruiting and onboarding them.

I had thought about all of this as I dialed Jim's phone number. Waiting for him to answer, my mind flashed through our process—the recruitment strategy was new, and the committee's composition and interview process were novel ideas, things the organization had not used before.

We'd spent more time in the interviews talking about values than competencies. We wanted to understand the quality of the people we were considering. During the meal with our short-listed candidates, we shared more life stories than professional anecdotes. We learned about the candidates and about each other too.

Changing how we hired had made an impact, validating the success of our values-led approach.

Closing Thoughts

Hire for heart and skill. Seek shared values. Nurture diversity and inclusion. Invest in people's development. By hiring and treating people right, you build an aligned, caring culture.

Whatever an employee's pay grade, the recruitment process is a two-way street. It is as critical that the candidate is sure they want to work at your organization as it is that the organization wants them on the team.

As leadership rock star Jim Collins writes, it's all about getting the right people on the bus,[129] and for me, it all starts with values: Do they align?

When the answer is yes, it's a cause for celebration. RSVP—attendees only—to chapter 11.

Key Takeaways

In this chapter, we've explored the importance of strategic hiring for cultural fit and creating a supportive work environment.

- Values alignment enables team cohesion.

- View employee recruitment as talent acquisition, an ongoing process.

- Leverage inclusive hiring to build diverse perspectives.

- Onboarding matters.

---

129 Collins, J. (2008). Good to great: Why some companies make the leap and others don't. HarperCollins.

For Reflection

Review your current hiring and onboarding practices. Identify two or three improvements to better assess values alignment and the integration of new hires into your organizational community.

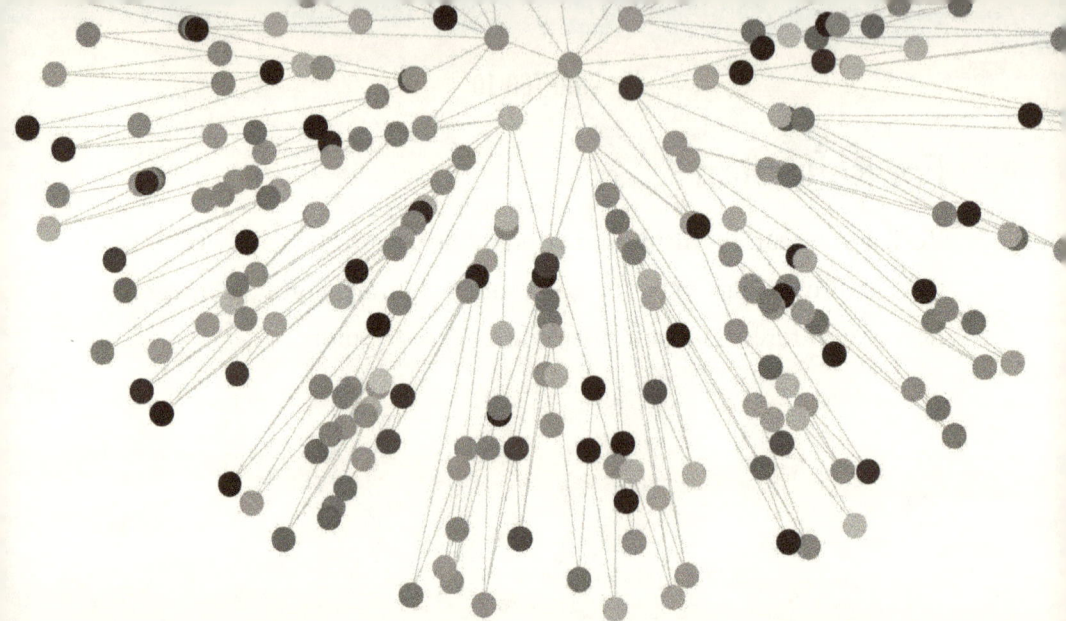

CHAPTER 11

COMMUNICATION AND CELEBRATION

One cannot not communicate.

—PAUL WATZLAWICK[130]

We gathered on the main stage of Protest U's spectacular, zillion-dollar performing arts center. There were no guitar solos. The only song heard that day was a well-known melody sung by all to our colleague Alan: "Happy Birthday."

A few dozen people filled the stage—it was a busy, buzzing place. When making the business case for this state-of-the-art facility, we hadn't included "staff birthday parties" as a prospective use.

But this was more—a special occasion for several reasons. As people wished Alan well, took helpings from the oversize cake, and

---

130 Watzlawick, P., Bavelas, J. B., & Jackson, D. D. (2011). *Pragmatics of human communication: A study of interactional patterns, pathologies and paradoxes.* W. W. Norton & Company.

mingled, I thought about how we'd gotten here. The day was for Alan, but this celebration was for all of us.

We'd come a long way from my first visit, interviewing for this gig as people protested on the concert hall's steps. We'd gone from an "us-versus-them" mindset to a "we" mindset. We'd become a community, but things didn't start that way.

Civil War

When I started my role as director of Protest U's conservatory of music, I learned there was tension between two opposing groups: those associated with curating the onstage talent and those who supported the facility and its events. At both teams' best, the conservatory's music staff were "roommates" with the performing arts center's technical staff. At their worst, they were straight-up adversaries.

The tensions had advanced to outright conflict. Like William Shakespeare's Montagues and Capulets, Waylon Jennings's Hatfields and McCoys, and Ross Geller's White Lab Coats and Blue Blazers, we were Protest U's Center-Stagers and Back-Stagers.

As leader of the Center-Stagers, my earliest conversations with faculty and staff featured tattling, as they pointed out all the Back-Stagers' "wrongdoings." When I met with the Back-Stagers' leadership team, they presented a laundry list of concerns and complaints against my team. The two sides were dug in pretty well, thanks in part to several years of strain.

How could I resolve this? How could we build community? The scenario was complex; many people were involved, including staff from another department. I acknowledged that a resolution would take time and committed to being patient and playing a long game.

As usual, I began with research, making myself visible, listening to hear, and reflection.

The roots of the tension, I learned, were claims that the performing arts center's financials were in the red. It seems the business case and financial forecasting had predicted immediate success, including programming growth for the conservatory and production success for the arts center, and thus, financial success for both.

When the first year's actuals did not align with expectations, tensions rose, and the finger-pointing began. It was the opposite of community. It was civil war.

In Alan We Trust

Alan wasn't management, but he was the most senior and most respected member of the Back-Stagers. He approached me one day and asked if we could chat. Surprised, as the Back-Stagers rarely talked to Center-Stagers, let alone Center-Stage management, I nonetheless agreed to a conversation.

We walked to the campus coffee shop (my second office), grabbed cups to go, and walked back to the concert hall's empty lobby.

Talking with Alan was easy. Years earlier, he had worked backstage at another venue where I had performed several times. He was great at his job, and we began with reminiscences of "the old days." Then, we got into the current state of affairs.

"People are so divided," he explained. "We've forgotten why we exist—to serve the arts community, to support it, to build it!" He was passionate.

"It's like, if I'm walking down the hall and I see that one of the conservatory's staff [a Center-Stager] has fallen and is lying on the ground, before I can help them up, I need to ask them where my time should be coded," he said, referring to the task-tracking system we used in the budgeting process.

His point was taken. Indeed, everyone had become focused on their budget centers, protecting their fragile accounts—it was the priority.

I recalled Mentor Mike's words: "When the watering hole starts shrinking, the animals start looking at each other differently." Our poor financials were the equivalent of a shrunken watering hole, and the Center-Stagers and Back-Stagers were certainly looking at each other differently. In such an adversarial environment, how could we repair, refocus, and build community?

Communication

In real estate, it's all about location, location, location. When building community, it's about communication, communication, communication.

I've mentioned my affection for Batman. Whether it's the classic TV version with Adam West, the cartoon version in *Super Friends*, or more recent cinematic incarnations, I'm interested.

Among the Caped Crusader's cool crime-fighting toys is his utility belt. Over the many reworkings of the superhero's adventures, the utility belt has remained constant. From it, the various Batmen have pulled everything from a grappling hook to scale tall buildings to shark-repellant spray. Somehow, that belt seems to have just what any situation calls for.

There are many ways a leader can communicate to build community, and no single one of them is better than another. Keep them all in your communication utility belt.

It's critical that people feel *a part* of, rather than *apart*. Armed with information, people are quicker to make both mental and emotional investments.

The link between communication, stakeholder motivation, and morale is irrefutable. The stories vary, yet every leadership post I've held has prioritized communication as a way to build community and enable success.

In my later twenties, I was elected president of the city's Guitar Society, and nobody was more surprised about it than I.

The group received funding from municipal and provincial government arts grants, along with local sponsors—businesses and individuals. Supporting our annual concert series, which brought in international rock stars, regional heroes, and emerging next-generation players, was not a problem, largely because attendance was usually decent.

Yet I noticed a lack of engagement with our community-building efforts, particularly outreach and educational events that promoted the instrument and fostered the next generation. In the president role, I addressed this by creating a city-wide newsletter (this was pre-social-media). The communication was welcomed, engagement grew, and our community formed.

At Faraway U, all employees received regular email updates. The purpose was transparency—to provide some details on how I spent my days—and to inform and (hopefully) inspire. I wanted employees to know what was happening in the organization and to share progress toward our goals, whether organizational successes or staff achievements.

But Dean Tanya took things to another level.

Tanya was a five-star communicator. *From the Dean's Desk* hit faculty and staff inboxes each Monday morning, informing all about and celebrating the week that was, while looking forward to the one ahead. The messages were professional yet personal. Tanya's portfolio was broad, and as a new manager, I appreciated learning what was happening across our faculty and felt pride at working in such a dynamic place.

"If you don't communicate," Tanya told me, "your employees will fill the gaps with their own stories."

Early in my director role at Protest U, I noticed that our music department's postsecondary folks didn't know what was happening with our preparatory and outreach programs. The folks who programmed our concert series often felt "alone on an island" too.

If we don't even know what's happening within our own department, I thought, *how can we share what's happening with the broader community?*

We started holding departmental huddles each Monday. The meetings never had an agenda, and we kept them to thirty minutes. We went around the table; people summarized the past week quickly, shared what was happening in their world this week, and asked for their colleagues' assistance if they anticipated a need.

Early in the process, colleagues with lighter weeks offered support to those with significant events on their calendars. But soon, I noticed a change.

As people shared the past week's adventures, they voiced gratitude for the support of their colleagues, often acknowledging specific individuals. As they turned to the coming week, they thanked people who *had already volunteered* to help fill in gaps.

Communication had gone viral and built camaraderie, which was broadening to cultivate community.

These meetings weren't held in a closed boardroom. We simply pulled chairs from offices and formed an imperfect circle in the lobby of our administrative HQ. When other faculty and staff wandered in, they were greeted with a wave and a smile and offered a muffin, cookie, or whatever we enjoyed that day.

Again, the goal was transparency, and the vibe was welcoming.

I supplemented these meetings with all-employee emails, sharing news and celebrating successes. The content was curated so messages could be forwarded to external stakeholders, or whomever people felt would appreciate the information.

The result: a community of colleagues.

State of the Union

American culture impacts Canada. Television, movies, music, sports, fashion, and other popular culture trends are infectious. US economic and political happenings also affect Canada and are typically absorbed through American media.

Teenage Brad was influenced by American rock music, but he found US politics equally fascinating. I loved LA hair metal and the president's State of the Union address.

My attraction to hair metal is likely obvious, but my draw to the commander in chief's annual address was a family tradition. We'd watch together as the president addressed significant issues facing Americans and offered ideas for managing them. Topics could also include accomplishments and appropriate celebrations.

Over the years, I noticed some presidents were more dynamic than others, but regardless, I always appreciated having their carefully considered perspectives.

So in my dean role, I added another layer to my comms utility belt: monthly "state of the union" updates. But with "state of the union" being somewhat taken, we called my monthly addresses "Coffee with Brad."

And the Oscar Goes to ...

The one-hour, in-person sessions were open to all employees. They began with mingling and casual socializing—a great chance for me to say hello to people I didn't always see day-to-day.

I followed with a verbal update, perhaps thirty minutes of information, then acknowledgments (which led to celebrations), and finally, to ensure a two-way dialogue, it was time for questions from the floor. But early on, the questions did not come.

In chapter 2, I noted that few want to question the boss, and fair enough—just put yourself in their shoes. I needed to earn trust by *proving* it was a safe space.

At an early Coffee with Brad, I planted a question with a willing staff member, Rick. He was a Green Bay Packers fan (his only fault). As previously disclosed, I'm a Chicago Bears fan. Given the teams' long rivalry, we had lots to talk about when we'd bump into each other around the building.

I asked if there were any questions, and Rick awkwardly raised his hand. I acted surprised and greeted his raised hand with enthusiasm.

Our skit was going perfectly.

"Yes, Rick!" I declared. "Please ask your question!" Rick pulled a piece of paper from his pocket and read a prepared question, which I eagerly answered, then thanked him—just a *little* too repeatedly—for the query.

Those in the crowd smiled; some chuckled. There'd be no Academy Award for our performance, but we did create the first question-answer moment and lightened the mood.

Then, another hand went up, and this time, it was no act. I again thanked my colleague for their question and fully engaged the topic before another hand went up—two "real" questions. In the months that followed, the question-answer period gradually grew to match the length of my presentation.

Our agenda usually concluded with about fifteen minutes remaining, a chance for staff to mingle a bit and discuss what they'd heard or to talk about whatever was on their minds. The informality of it allowed me to be visible and connect more fully, with coffee, tea, juice, and snacks provided. I've always believed that "breaking bread" with colleagues is healthy. At a more basic level, food and drink draw people in.

Then the budget cuts came. Senior admin suspended all hospitality around food-and-beverage purchases, which meant the "coffee" in Coffee with Brad was no more.

Spies confirmed that employees were concerned about the cuts—and not the drinks and snacks at my monthly addresses. They feared layoffs.

Hood (2018) writes about the "importance of open communication,"[131] so we took the opportunity to call an important all-staff meeting, rebranded Tap Water with Brad. The tongue-in-cheek title aimed to lower the temperature around budget cuts, but the open communication is what truly addressed and alleviated employees' concerns.

Leadership superhero John C. Maxwell's words came to me: "The most powerful leadership tool is communication."[132] It was also our tool of choice in addressing our organization's greatest unknown: COVID-19.

During the global pandemic, we pivoted to weekly online meetings—rebranded once more, this time as Social Distancing with

---

131   Hood, S. (2018). The business of people. *HR Magazine.*

132   Maxwell, J. C. (2007). *The 21 irrefutable laws of leadership: Follow them and people will follow you.* HarperCollins Leadership.

Brad. The goal was unchanged: **communication, celebration, connection, and community**.

Though tales of feeling isolated pervaded the news, our faculty's bond seemed to strengthen, not diminish. It was testament to our employees' engagement and the strength of our community.

When addressing employees, I'd often share tidbits about my personal and family life. I never forced it but took the opportunities when they came. It proved to be another path to connection and community, opening to staff the chance to share a bit about themselves too.

The better we knew each other, the better we understood each other, the better we worked together.

But have no illusions: building a community when colleagues work in isolation is quite challenging. In my president role at Grasslands, our six campus regions covered one hundred thousand square kilometers. So I began sharing photos of my travels in mass employee emails and posted some to our social media channels. Virtual state-of-the-union addresses (called Brews with Brad) with Q-and-A sessions intact continued, resulting in awareness and appreciation of what was happening across our vast service area.

Like my EQ radar, my communication utility belt was always on by engaging in emails, hallway conversations, and live and virtual state-of-the-union addresses. Building on chapter 9, these communications allowed me to model behavior, because **employees always watch you**.

On with the Show

Thanks to Alan's ice-breaking, I soon started meeting with the Back-Stagers' management team. It started with a few coffees, which evolved into lunches, which led to the occasional after-hours beverage. We got to know each other as people and leaders and gave voice to our values and vision.

Leadership guru Stephen Covey reminds us that effective communication is essential for building trust and understanding in any organization.[133] As we communicated deliberately, our understanding of each other grew. Trust was building.

We shared what we had learned from each other with our respective teams. That sent a crucial, broader message to staff: Center-Stage management and Back-Stage management were communicating.

Texas A&M University business professor David Griffith outlines the importance of effective communication, calling it a critical component of a successful business strategy, including relationship building.[134] Our communications had built a foundation for our relationship.

Next, I invited a Back-Stage manager to our Center-Stage team meeting. The Back-Stagers reciprocated; I attended their department meeting to share information and to learn firsthand.

Writer, psychotherapist, and philosopher Rollo Reece May says communication leads to community, which is understanding, intimacy, and mutual valuing.[135] Our experiment went well; communication was connecting our departments and cultivating community. As trust grew, we began sending one or two department reps—instead of management—as guests to the meetings. Citing Covey again, when the trust account is high, communication is easy, instant, and effective.[136]

A community was forming.

133 Covey, S. R. (2020). *The 7 habits of highly effective people.* Simon & Schuster.

134 Griffith, D. A. (2002). The role of communication competencies in international business relationship development. *Journal of World Business,* 37(4), 256–265.

135 May, R. (1969). *Love and will.* W. W. Norton & Company.

136 Covey, "The 7 Habits."

Staff and management from both camps were hearing perspectives they never had before. Increasingly, those of the other departments were heard too. We didn't always agree, but we'd opened a clear and respectful line of communication among staff, and it had started with leadership.

With time, it became normal to see Center- and Back-Stagers talking in the concert hall lobby, the hallways, even in each other's offices.

As another year passed, we saw program growth and concert attendance more reflective of the original business plan's projections. We still weren't where we needed to be, but our progress was obvious. It was a win.

Another year and still more progress led to Protest U's senior admin nominating the Center-Stagers and Back-Stagers for the university's Effective Team Award at the annual employee appreciation event.

We won!

We'd created an internal community, and together, we served our external community. The catalysts: communication and celebration.

Over the years, I've been fortunate to collect a few awards and parchments. The Effective Team Award is still on display in my office.

Closing Thoughts

Of all the leadership tools, **communication is among the most critical**. Voicing your values and vision, keeping stakeholders informed, and celebrating successes all contribute to cultivating community. And community fosters a culture of shared ownership and investment in organizational success.

WE'D CREATED AN INTERNAL COMMUNITY, AND TOGETHER, WE SERVED OUR EXTERNAL COMMUNITY.

Communication and celebration motivate people. Share news persistently. Discuss strategy transparently. Make time for dialogue. Recognize accomplishments. Foster fun and camaraderie. Through regular updates and celebrating wins, teams unite to produce results.

Key Takeaways

In this chapter, we explored the power of frequent updates and celebrating achievements in motivating and unifying teams.

- Communication drives motivation.

- Celebration unifies teams.

- Updates and recognition boost morale.

For Reflection

Audit your current communication practices and recognition programs. Identify and champion two or three improvements to increase transparency, dialogue, and celebration.

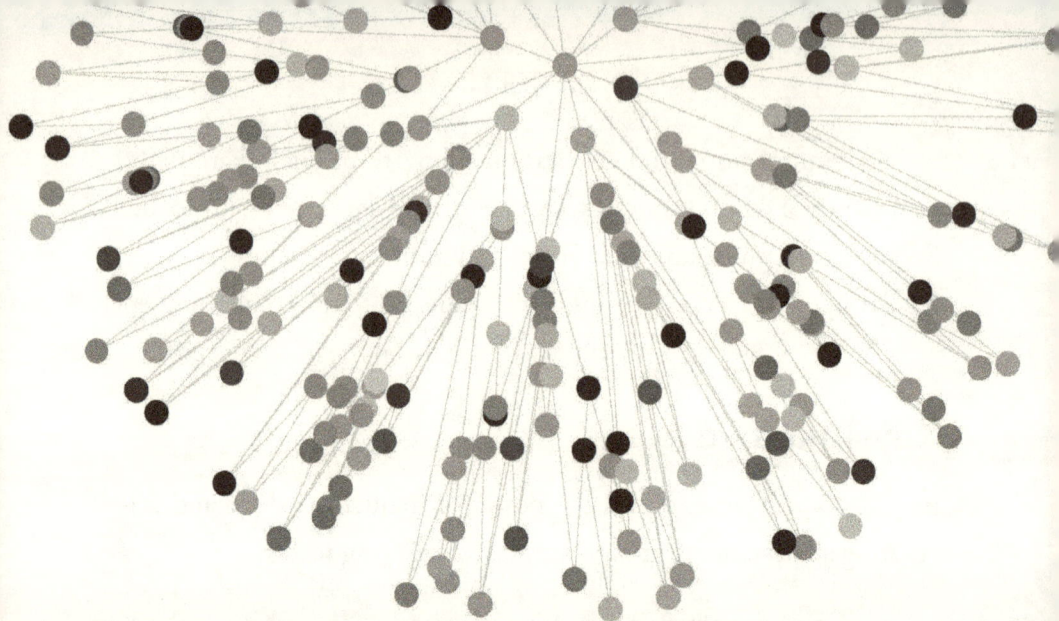

CONCLUSION

THE ENGAGEMENT ADVANTAGE

Success is a team sport.

—SIMON SENEK[137]

It was President Brad's third season (one last sports analogy; I couldn't resist).

Nearly five years after COVID-19 shut the world down, one of our campus communities was at last hosting a real (versus virtual) trade show, in partnership with the local chamber of commerce. People were excited, and the conference center buzzed with activity.

I was there, of course.

Besides reinforcing our partnership with the chamber, my visibility allowed me to connect with business owners, community

---

137   Sinek, S. (2009). *Start with why: How great leaders inspire everyone to take action.* Penguin.

leaders, and elected officials. I also dropped in to visit with staff at our college booth.

I stood behind the table as the sea of people shuffled by. Most looked at us, at the signage bearing our brand, back to us, then a smile, then they'd carry on. After some time, I leaned over to my colleague, who'd been at our booth for the entire event.

"How's it been going?" I asked.

She started to speak, then paused and thought. "There's been lots of traffic but not much interaction." I nodded, and before I could reply, she continued. "But you know, that doesn't matter; this event is important to the community, so we need to be here."

Realization struck, leaving me speechless: Those are *my* key messages! Staff are getting it—*they're buying in*!

There was further evidence.

Remember Hazlet and the par-three golf tournament? Since I spent that first lonely year dodging golf balls while ensuring the integrity of the hole-in-one prize, carloads of my colleagues now travel to support the event—we have staff *at every hole*.

And then there were the parades.

What started with a few spirited lone wolves (and sometimes, just me), has become a team-building, community-engaging celebration! Staff, students, and eventually their family members—indeed, our entire internal campus community—*wanted* to walk beside our oversize red truck. There was *pride*, and it showed.

Baton Life

The orchestral conductor has always fascinated me. They wave their wand and create magic. I've also seen them struggle as the train came off the tracks. There may not be a purer leadership role.

They are critical players. Despite lacking an instrument, their contribution impacts success or failure. It's about *how* they lead, which begins in the auditions, continues in rehearsals, and culminates in concert.

Leonard Bernstein is often considered one of the twentieth century's great conductors. His passion for his art was contagious, inspiring engagement from musicians and audiences alike.[138] The community he cultivated—how he made those under his baton and those listening and watching *feel*—is part of his celebrated legacy.

This realization has been a touchstone of my leadership journey. I am never the marketing expert in the room, the financial guru, or the technology genius, but I do need to unite these diverse personalities to create a team and to guide it toward a shared North Star.

Reflecting on my lived experiences, every success has had one common denominator: community engagement, both internal and external. It is the source of programming innovation, expanded partnerships, heightened brand recognition, reputation enhancement, increased enrollments, improved financial positions, a strong internal culture, broader facility usage, and invested external stakeholders.

It all begins with getting out there—and bringing your values with you.

CEO: Chief *Engagement* Officer

Cultivating community connections generates concrete payoffs. The principles in these pages apply widely to businesses of varying sizes, in diverse sectors.

Competitive advantage flows from the community you identify, participate in, help build, and ultimately serve—making that

138   Shawn, A. (2014). *Leonard Bernstein: An American musician.* Yale University Press.

community your full partner. That starts with leadership, and leadership starts within.

Years of steering higher education and arts organizations have taught me that authentic, purpose-driven leadership requires self-awareness, emotional intelligence, and values, which guide your vision.

- Know yourself first. Your values must shape your vision.

- Lead with heart and see the humanity in every person.

- Understand your neighbors and forge win-win partnerships.

- An open door invites people in.

- Model desired behaviors.

- Hire those who share your values.

- Communicate with transparency.

- Recognize achievements.

- Align your actions to support the community you serve.

At its core, leadership is a personal journey of self-discovery, learning to connect, and building partnerships.

Wherever your leadership path takes you, it is my sincere hope that you find your authentic self and lead your teams to become more purposeful and impactful than they ever thought possible.